SELECTED POEMS

FORD MADOX FORD (the name he adopted in 1919: he was originally Ford Hermann Hueffer) was born in Merton, Surrey, in 1873. His mother, Catherine, was the daughter of the Pre-Raphaelite painter Ford Madox Brown. His father, Francis Hueffer, was a German émigré: a musicologist and music critic for *The Times*. Christina and Dante Gabriel Rossetti were his aunt and uncle by marriage. Ford collaborated with Conrad from 1898 to 1908, and also befriended many of the best writers of his time, including James, Wells, Crane, Galsworthy, and Hardy. He is best known for his novels; especially *The Fifth Queen* (a trilogy about Henry VIII; 1906-8); *The Good Soldier* (1915); and *Parade's End* (the tetralogy about the First World War, in which he served). He was also an influential poet, critic, and editor. He founded the *English Review* in 1908, publishing Lawrence, Wyndham Lewis, and Pound, who became another close friend. In post-war Paris he founded *the transatlantic review*, taking on Hemingway as a sub-editor, discovering Rhys and Bunting, and publishing Joyce and Stein. In the 1920s and 1930s he moved between Paris, New York, and Provence. He died in Deauville in June 1939. The author of over eighty books, Ford is a major presence in twentieth-century writing.

MAX SAUNDERS is Professor of English at King's College London, where he teaches modern English and Comparative Literature. He studied at the universities of Cambridge and Harvard, and was a Research Fellow and then College Lecturer at Selwyn College Cambridge. He is the author of *Ford Madox Ford: A Dual Life* (2 vols, Oxford: Oxford University Press, 1996), and the editor of Ford's *War Prose* (Carcanet Press, 1999) and *Critical Essays* (with Richard Stang, Carcanet Press, 2002). He has published essays on Ford, Eliot, Joyce, Rosamond Lehmann, Lawrence, Freud, Pound, Ruskin, and others.

Fyfield*Books* aim to make available some of the great classics of British and European literature in clear, affordable formats, and to restore often neglected writers to their place in literary tradition.

Fyfield*Books* take their name from the Fyfield elm in Matthew Arnold's 'Scholar Gypsy' and 'Thyrsis'. The tree stood not far from the village where the series was originally devised in 1971.

Roam on! The light we sought is shining still.
Dost thou ask proof? Our tree yet crowns the hill,
Our Scholar travels yet the loved hill-side

from 'Thyrsis'

FORD MADOX FORD

Selected Poems

Edited with an introduction by
MAX SAUNDERS

Fyfield*Books*

CARCANET

First published in Great Britain in 1997 by
Carcanet Press Limited
Alliance House
Cross Street
Manchester M2 7AQ

This impression 2003

Selection, introduction and editorial matter © Max Saunders 1997, 2003
Poems by Ford Madox Ford © Michael Schmidt 1997, 2003

A CIP catalogue record for this book is available from the British Library
ISBN 1 85754 713 6

The publisher acknowledges financial assistance from Arts Council England

Printed and bound in England by SRP Ltd, Exeter

CONTENTS

Poets or novelists tend also to be our best critics: Coleridge, Arnold, Eliot, Pound and Empson; or James, Nabokov and Woolf. It's much rarer to find major novelists who are also major poets: Goethe; Emily Brontë; Victor Hugo; Hardy; perhaps Poe. Rarer still are writers who change the course of all three genres: Dr Johnson; Wilde, perhaps; certainly Lawrence; and also Ford Madox Ford. Ford will always be read primarily for his novels, particularly his masterpieces *The Good Soldier* and *Parade's End*. But he was also a gifted poet and critic, and surprisingly influential in both fields.

His constant champion, Ezra Pound, praised him in 1913 as 'the best critic in England, one might say the only critic of any importance', and also said: 'we would not be far wrong in calling Mr Hueffer the best lyrist in England'. He hailed Ford's long poem of the following year, 'On Heaven', as 'the best poem yet written in the "twentieth-century fashion"'. Our sense of what a modernist meant by the 'twentieth-century fashion' has been shaped by subsequent landmarks: 'Prufrock', 'Hugh Selwyn Mauberley', and *The Waste Land*. For Pound, Ford's example as poet-critic helped make modernist poetry possible, energising its rigour and verbal intelligence, exploring the potential of free verse.

When Ford was living in Germany, in 1911, Pound visited, and worked as his secretary. He said that when he produced a copy of his latest volume, Ford 'felt the errors of contemporary style' to the point of rolling on the floor in front of him. It was the 'stilted language' he couldn't stand. Pound took his humiliation gratefully (if not humbly), and said 'that roll saved me at least two years, perhaps more. It sent me back to my own proper effort, namely, toward using the living tongue (with younger men after me), though none of us has found a more natural language than Ford did'. He took up Ford's slogans that 'poetry should be at least as well-written as prose, and that "good prose is just your conversation"', as well as his idea that descriptions of objects could be expressive of unstated emotions; and he spread Ford's influence to other poets such as Yeats (who had admired the 'right lyrical vehemence' of his first book of poems) and Eliot (who called the poem on Antwerp 'the only good poem I have met with on the subject of the war'). It wasn't only Pound who recognised Ford as 'The man who did the *work* for English writing'. Other poets among his admirers include Allen Tate, W.H. Auden, Robert Lowell, Basil Bunting, William Carlos Williams, Donald Davie, Charles Tomlinson, and C.H. Sisson. The list of novelists would be longer.

The problem with the Poundian view of Ford – apart from his neglect of the novels – is that it limits Fordian poetics to what Pound needed to learn from him, and misses the range, development, and some of the crucial strengths of the poetry. It was between Ford's major nervous breakdown of 1904, and his meeting with Pound in 1909, that his verse evolved from wistful pastorals in the manner of his aunt (by marriage), Christina Rossetti, or of Housman, to the conversational impressionism that Pound admired. The language is natural and living in both modes. But the earlier verse was often written for setting to music, and often was set by Ford himself (whose phenomenal versatility had also let him consider becoming a composer). A manuscript version of one of his early volumes, *The Face of the Night*, is headed 'Poems in Two Keys (Little Plays and Poems for Music)'; and the two previous volumes have subtitles describing some of the poems as 'for notes of music'. Between his founding of *The English Review* in 1908, and the First World War, however, Ford moved closer towards an ideal of poetry as quiet talk, intimate conversation. It is a shift which corresponds to the way he was modernising himself in his fiction, too, as he abandoned the Pre-Raphaelite overload of period detail of his historical romances such as the *Fifth Queen* trilogy, in favour of the modern subjects, more conversational styles, and greater technical complexities, of *The Good Soldier* and *Parade's End*.

It is the conversational quality of Ford's poetry that has continued to be most admired. Robert Lowell praised the last group of poems, *Buckshee*, thus: 'In these reveries, he has at last managed to work his speaking voice, and something more than his speaking voice, into poems – the inner voice of the tireless old man, the old master still in harness, confiding, tolerant, Bohemian, newly married, and in France'. Ford's word for that writer's inner voice was 'cadence': the characteristic curve of an author's sentence. His own voice (which his youngest daughter likened to Charles Laughton's) had a poignant, dying fall, omniscient, wryly stoical.

The two *Collected Poems* Ford published, in 1913 and 1936, compounded the difficulties of gauging his poetic *œuvre*. The first reverses the chronological order of composition; the second disrupts it. The present selection restores it, in order to make his development more visible. Ford's collections also exclude some of the best examples of his other great strength as a poet, satirical irony. This is the other major quality that the Poundian view of Ford's poetry misses (which is odd, given his admiration for Ford's prose satires like *Mr Fleight*, and the fact that it is the mode in which his own best verse before *The Cantos* excels – what he called 'the dance of the intellect among words').

When Ford planned a second collection of poems in the late 1920s, he thought of including the bizarre virtuoso dramatic poem he had published in 1923 with illustrations by Paul Nash. The full title gives an idea of its innovatory panache: *Mister Bosphorus and the Muses or a Short History of Poetry in Britain. Variety Entertainment in Four Acts . . . with Harlequinade, Transformation Scene, Cinematograph Effects, and Many Other Novelties, as well as Old and Tried Favourites*. It isn't known why it was eventually excluded. Perhaps Ford had doubts about it; perhaps its 126 pages told against it. Unfortunately it is only possible to offer an extract here, to give an indication of the vigour and mordancy of his satiric vein. Another important but uncollected poem from the same post-war phase is included here in its entirety: 'Immortality'. Like *Mr Bosphorus*, it can be read as a fantasy to avenge his literary neglect at the time (just before the novels of *Parade's End* began to re-make his reputation). But it also engages importantly with his feelings about writers he had befriended – especially James and Conrad; and – again like *Mr Bosphorus* – with more general problems about the human cost of art, and the relation between art and love. Ford's satiric talent is also evident in the earlier poem (which he did collect), 'Süssmund's Address To An Unknown God', which purports to be an adaptation from the 'High German' of a fictional baronial alter-ego (with 'Süssmund' perhaps echoing the Middle High German poet Süsskind von Trimberg, but translating ironically as 'sweet-mouth').

These two kinds of misrepresentation only partly explain why Ford's poetry is not as well-known as it deserves to be. The main problem has been availability. His mature *Collected Poems* was never published in Britain; the publishers delayed, then the war intervened. He has been better served in America, where Robert Lowell and Kenneth Rexroth produced an edition of the *Buckshee* poems in 1966, and Basil Bunting edited a slim selection in 1971. That a major modernist such as Ford still needs a *Complete Poems* is something of a scandal, but entirely typical of his posthumous fate in his own century. The Carcanet 'Millennium Ford' project at last offers the prospect of a serious revaluation.

Bunting identified three reasons why he didn't dare maintain Ford's greatness as a poet. First, the impressionism developed with Conrad. Though they advocated a Flaubertian pursuit of *le mot juste*, Bunting argues that they 'surrounded their meaning with successive approximations instead, and so repeated in the texture of prose the pattern by which their narrative captured their theme'. This 'circuitous' technique deals with 'nebulosities and imprecisions' which 'are much of our landscape without or within, and worth reproducing'. Bunting says Ford reproduces them in his best poems. But his faint praise betrays a modernist impatience with discursive forms, and with the impressionist preoccupation with modes of perception.

This criticism leads him onto the other two: a charge of sentimentality (or 'prettification'); and of Pre-Raphaelite pastiche. Sentiment and pastiche are crucial issues for Ford's poetics. But for the most part they are very different in his writing from the kind of Pre-Raphaelite haziness Bunting decries. If his emotions occasionally make us wince, it is because they are naked, not draped in cliché; it is because he is not afraid to express emotions we have generally been taught not to express – self-pity, morbidity, wish-fulfilment, persecutory anxiety, nostalgia, sadness and despair. The pathos of 'Antwerp', for example, might seem mawkish now – though Conrad Aiken thought it 'one of the three or four brilliant poems inspired by the war'. John Peale Bishop described how Ford's best poems give 'a record of his own emotions' which 'is meant, too, to record the contemporary world; which is so realistic on the surface, so romantic in its depths'. But this raises the other issue: can poetry record the contemporary if it draws upon pastiche of the old? Ford's criticism implies it cannot. He often recalled his father's critique of Rossetti's style, 'which a poet of Dante's age might have used if he had been able to read Shakespeare'. 'We wait', Ford argued in 1905, 'for the poet who, in limpid words, with clear enunciation and, without inverted phrases, shall give the mind of the time sincere frame and utterance.' To his Edwardian contemporaries he seemed to be that poet. Yet to post-war ears, his practice seems haunted by the minds of earlier times. The question matters, because Ford's verve in pastiche is something central to his verse, not merely a danger lying at the margins. Nor does he limit himself to Victorian pastiche. This volume resounds with echoes of Greek tragedy, Old Testament prophecy, Minnesingers, Troubadours, Renaissance lyrics, rural dialect, Shakespeare, Browning, Pound, music hall, and of Ford himself. Like Joyce, Ford found his individuality through parody and pastiche. And this is why he can now sometimes (like Joyce and Eliot) seem a premature post-modernist writer, rather than a compromised modernist. Pastiche can express the contemporary world when that world is perceived as itself operating according to received discourses; that is, as itself already pastiche. Here Ford is truly Flaubertian, registering an ironic self-consciousness of the clichés the Edwardian mind could not do without.

It may be that his criticism urges relinquishing anachronism *because* he found it so hard to escape in his own writing; because his habitual mode is neither exclusively anachronising nor exclusively modernising, but a juxtaposing of past and present. Some intriguing poems included here show the two modes in tension, as a modernised colloquial urban realism ironises the arcadian-pastoral voice: 'Castles in the Fog' (later re-titled as 'Finchley Road'); and 'The Three-Ten'. They could be read as transitional moments between a Pre-Raphaelite Ford and a modernist one. Or their tonal duality could be seen as characteristic of his entire *œuvre*. After all, the novels too negotiate between the past and present, whether rendering the Middle Ages with a modern disabused psychological realism, or twentieth-century characters in the grip of feudal or eighteenth-century Tory principles and romance sentiments.

Most accounts of Ford's poetics have located his significance in the transformation of diction and imagery. This follows his own emphasis on these things. In his influential preface to the 1913 *Collected Poems* he argued that 'the business of poetry is not sentimentalism so much as the putting of certain realities in certain aspects'; and that 'the real stuff of the poetry of our day' was to be found in 'the portable zinc dustbin left at dawn for the dustman to take', rather than 'the comfrey under the hedge': contemporary urban social facts, rather than pastoral convention. Such were the campaigns that seemed decisive to the Imagists and Vorticists of pre-war London. Yet they neglect what may be Ford's more lastingly significant mastery: his handling of verse forms and sentence structures. For the conversational style is as much a matter of getting individual words to sound naturally within a sentence, and of getting a sentence to fall naturally in a stanza, as it is a matter of choosing a contemporary word instead of an archaic one. It is the quality Bunting admired, saying of Ford's best poems: 'Any poet should study their management' not only of 'diction', but of 'rhythm and narrative'. Lowell, too, recognised it. He said Ford 'had a religious fascination in the possibilities of sentence structure and fictional techniques.' And though he was thinking primarily of the novels, the structures and techniques of the poems are admirable, too. However, as with Ford's prose, it is often the masterly unobtrusiveness of his effects that lets readers ignore them. The clarity of 'A House', for example, makes it seem deceptively simple, distracting us from the originality of its masque-like or dream-like form, and the exquisite tonal effects created by the variations in line-lengths:

> *The Tree.* I am the great Tree over above this House!
>   I resemble
>   The drawing of a child. Drawing 'just a tree'
>   The child draws Me!

Heavy leaves, old branches, old knots:
I am more old than the house is old.
I have known nights so cold
I used to tremble;
For the sap frozen in my branches,
And the mouse,
That stored her nuts in my knot-holes, died. I am strong
Now . . . Let a storm come wild
Over the Sussex Wold,
I no longer fear it.
I have stood too long!

'A House' was awarded the $100 prize by the Chicago-based *Poetry* magazine that published it, for the best poem of 1921. Or take the vignettes of soldiers in the Welch Regiment. 'Regimental Records' makes from syntax music as captivating as the men's feelings it describes:

'And so her quiet eyes ensnare
My eyes all day and fill my sense
And take
My thoughts all day away from other things; and keep
Me, when I should be fast asleep,
Awake!'

Ford had too much facility to need to labour over verse. He can express complex ideas in complex forms that unfold effortlessly, as if perfectly improvised. The poignancy and tenderness he achieves here, or in the first three lyrics of the selection, or in the poem he said was his favourite – 'When the World Was in Building' – or in his last poem – the magnificent 'Coda' – are evidence of his remarkable talent. His virtuosity wasn't practised for its own sake. 'All Art of course is just a means of expression. It is the way in which one human soul expresses itself to – or in the alternative – conceals itself from, other human beings'. That paradox of expression and concealment is at the heart of Ford's aesthetics, which are often a matter of expressing *through* concealment, understatement, suppression (hence those characteristic dots . . .). 'The Starling', for example, works by an oddly expressive, anti-Romantic disjunction between the visualised scene and the articulated voice. Ultimately, the impression left by his cadences, whether lyrical or conversational, is of a personality. As he put it in his lecture-notes from the 1920s on *vers libre*: 'however you [. . .] phrase your thoughts to yourself, the rhythm of your thought phrases will be your personality. It will be your literary personality . . . your true one'.

The texts of the poems printed here are of the first known published versions, unless otherwise annotated. Many of the poems were revised extensively. Some personal passages, and idiosyncrasies of ideas and expression were removed. The earlier punctuation tends to indicate musical phrasing rather than logical or syntactical structure. Occasional printers' errors have been silently corrected. Revised titles are given in square brackets after the original ones. Most of the poems were included by Ford in one or both of his *Collected Poems*, except those indicated as follows:

*   published in one of Ford's volumes of verses, but excluded from both *Collected Poems*
†   published in a periodical but not included in any of Ford's volumes of verse
‡   not published by Ford.

Acknowledgements

I am very grateful to Sara Haslam, Bill Hutchings, Penny Jones, Robyn Marsack, Ignazia Posadinu, and Harold Short, for their help with the preparation of this volume.

                                                              – MAX SAUNDERS

THE WIND'S QUEST[1]

'Oh where shall I find rest? – '
Sighed the Wind from the West,
'I've sought in vale o'er dale and down,
Through tangled woodland, tarn and town,
But found no rest.'

'Rest thou ne'er shall find – '
Answered Love to the Wind,
'For thou and I, and the great, grey sea
May never rest till Eternity
Its end shall find.'

SONG DIALOGUE

'Is it so, my dear?'
    'Even so!'
'Too much woe to bear?'
    'Too much woe!'
'Wait a little while,
We must bear the whole,
Do not weep, but smile,
We are near the goal.'

'Is it dark – the night?'
    'Very dark!'
'Not a spark of light?'
    'Not a spark!'
'Yet a little way
We must journey on;
Night will turn to day
And the goal be won.'

---

[1] Text taken from *The Questions At The Well*

'Will the dawn come soon?'
    'In an hour;
See! the sinking moon
    Loses power.
Saffron grey the West
Wakes before the sun.
Very soon we'll rest
Now that day's begun.'

IN TENEBRIS

All within is warm,
    Here without it's very cold,
    Now the year is grown so old
And the dead leaves swarm.

In your heart is light,
    Here without it's very dark
    Tired with woe and weary cark?
When shall I see aright?

Oh, for a moment's space!
    Draw the clinging curtains wide
    Whilst I wait and yearn outside
Let the light fall on my face.

SEA JEALOUSY

Cast not your looks upon the wan grey sea,
Waste not your voice upon the wind:
Let not your footsteps sink upon the sand,
Hold no sea-treasure in your hand,
And let no sea-shell in your ear
Nor any sea-thought in your mind
Murmur a mystery.

Turn your soft eyes upon mine eyes that long,
Let your sweet lips on mine be sealed;
Fold soft sweet hands upon your sweet soft breasts
And, as a weary sea-mew rests
Upon the sea,
Utterly, utterly yield
Your being up to me,
And all around grey seascape and the sound
Of droned sea song.

A NIGHT PIECE

As I lay awake by my good wife's side
And heard the clock measure a night of June,
I thought of a song and a haunting tune.
– But the thoughts that betide
And the songs that we hear in the ear when the June moon rides in the sky,
Fade and die –
Fade and die away at the coming of the day,
At the waning and fading and sinking of the moon. –

And the haloed angels with golden wings,
And the small sweet bells that rang in tune,
And the strings that quivered beneath the quills,
And all my mellow imaginings,
Faded and died away at the coming of the day
With the gradual growth and spread of grey above the hills.

LOVE IN WATCHFULNESS ON THE SHEEPDOWNS
[LOVE IN WATCHFULNESS UPON THE SHEEPDOWNS]

Sail, oh sail away,
Oh sail, you clouds, above my face
Here where I lie.
Trail, oh trail away,
Oh you minutes, and give place
To hours that fly.
Up here I've watched the road
And seen the shadows play
Half the day.
Oh, when I hear an echo mutter
Soft up the slope of gorse's gold,
I shall hear my heart a-flutter:
Oh, when I see a distant kerchief spread,
And see a spot of white beyond the farthest fold,
And see the sheep all scattered at his tread,
Above the shrouds
And gliding veils of mist, above my head,
You'll trail away,
You hours and clouds.

ENOUGH

'Enough for you,' said he, 'that ye from afar have viewed this goodly
thing that all that many may never espy.' – *How they Quested, etc.*

Long we'd sought for Avalon,
Avalon the rest place;
Long, long we'd laboured
The oars – yea for years.

Late, late one eventide
Saw we o'er still waters
Turrets rise and roof frets
Golden in a glory,
Heard for a heart-beat
Women choirs and harpings
Waft down the wave-ways.

Saw we long-sought Avalon
Sink thro' still waters –
Long, long we'd laboured
The oars – yea, and yearned.

AFTER ALL

Yes, what's the use of striving on?
And what's to show when all is done?
The bells will toll as now they toll,
Here's an old lilt will summarise the whole:

'This fell about in summertide,
About the midmost of the year,
Our master did to covert ride
To drive the fallow deer.
Chanced we upon the Douglas' men ere ever one of us was ware.

'Then sped a shaft from covert side
And piercèd in behind his ear;
This fell about in summertide
At midmost of the year.'

So down he fell and rested there
Among the sedge hard by the brook,
About the midmost of the year
His last and lasting rest he took.

And so, *'This fell in winter late,*
Or ever Candlemas grew near,
His bride had found another mate
Before the ending of the year.
His goshawks decked another's wrists, his hounds another's voice did fear.
His men another's errands ride,
His steed another burden bear,
Him they forgot by Christmastide,
Ere Candlemas drew near.'

Our hounds shall know another leash, *our* men another master know,
And we reck little of it all, so we but find good rest below.

So what's the use of striving on?
And what's to show when all is done?
The ring of bells will chime and chime,
And all the rest's just waste – just waste of time.

THE OLD FAITH TO THE CONVERTS

'When the world is growing older,
And the road leads down and down and down,
And the wind is in the bare tree-tops,
And the meadows sodden with much rain,
Seek me here in the old places,
And here, where I dwell, you shall find me,'
Says the old Faith we are leaving.

'When the muscles stiffen,
Eyes glaze, ears lose their keenness,
When the mind loses its familiar nimbleness,
And the tongue no longer voices it, speeds before it, follows it,
Seek me here in the old places,
And here, where I have always dwelt, you shall find me,'
Says the old Faith we are leaving.

'I shall not watch your going down the road,
Not even to the turning at the hill,
Not for me to hear you greet the strange women,
Not for me to see them greet you.
They shall be many and many the houses you shall enter,
    but never shall house be like to mine,'
Says the old Faith we are leaving.

'You shall hear strange new songs, but never song like
    the one I sing by your pillow;
You shall breathe strange new scents, but never scent
    like that of the herbs I strew 'mid the linen.

Go! I give you time to make holiday, travel, travel, fare into far countries,
But you shall come back again to the old places,
And here, where I have always dwelt, you shall find me,'
Says the old Faith we are leaving.

But we – we shall never return.

IN ADVERSITY*

'Cold hands, warm heart?'
Then let the wind blow chill
On our clasped hands who fare across the hill.
'Hard lot, hot love?'
Then let our pathway go
Through lone grey lands, knee-deep amid the snow.

A LULLABY

We've wandered all about the upland fallows,
　　We've watched the rabbits at their play;
　But now, good-night, good-bye to soaring swallows,
　　Now, good-night, good-bye, dear day.
Poppy heads are closing fast, pigeons circle home at last;
　　Sleep, baby, sleep, the bats are calling;
Pansies never miss the light, but sweet babes must sleep at night;
　　Sleep, baby, sleep, the dew is falling.

　Even the wind among the whisp'ring willows
　　Rests, and the waves are resting too.
　See, soft white linen; cool, such cool white pillows
　　Wait in the darkling room for you.
All the little lambs are still, now the moon peeps down the hill;
　　Sleep, Liebchen, sleep, the owls are hooting;
Ships have hung their lanthorns out, little mice dare creep about;
　　Sleep, Liebchen, sleep, the stars are shooting.

THE CUCKOO AND THE GYPSY
[THE GYPSY AND THE CUCKOO][1]

JASPER: 'We are not miserable, brother.'

ROMANY RYE: 'Well, then, you ought to be, Jasper. Have you an inch of ground your own? Are you of the least use? Are you not spoken ill of by everybody? What is a gipsy?'

JASPER: 'What's that bird noising yonder?'

ROMANY RYE: 'The bird! Oh, that's a cuckoo tolling; but what has the cuckoo to do with the matter?'

Tell me, brother, what's a cuckoo, but a roguish chaffing bird;
 Not a nest's its own, no bough-rest's its own,
And it's never man's good word,
But its call is musical
 And rings pleasant on the ear,
And the spring would scarce be spring
If the cuckoo did not sing
 In the leafy months o' the year.

Tell me, brother, what's a gipsy, but a roguish chaffing chap?
 Not a cat his own, not a man would groan
For a gipsy's worst mishap;
 But his tent looks quaint when bent
On the side-sward of a lane,
 And the rain might seem more dreary
 And the long white road more weary
If we never came again.

Would your May days seem more fair
 Were we chals deep-read in books,
 Were we cuckoos cawing rooks,
 All the brakes cathedral closes
 Where the very sunlight dozes,
Were the sounds all organ tone and book and bell and prayer?

---

[1] Ford later substituted the following epigraph:

'Brother, what's that bird tolling yonder?'
'Why, Jasper, that's a cuckoo.'
'He's a roguish chaffing sort of bird, isn't he, brother?'
'He is, Jasper.'
'But you rather like him, brother? . . . Well, brother, and what's a gipsy?'
– *The Romany Rye*.

THE GIPSY AND THE TOWNSMAN:
A DIALOGUE-PENDANT TO 'THE GIPSY AND THE CUCKOO'

The Townsman:
Pleasant enough in the seed-time;
Pleasant enough in the hay-time;
Pleasant enough in the grain-time;
When woods don golden gowns.
But the need-time –
The grey-time –
The rain-time –
How bear ye them,
How fare ye then,
When the rain-clouds sweep over the gorse on the downs –
How bear ye them, how fare ye then?

The Gipsy:
We lie round the fire and we hark to the wind,
As it wails in the gorse and whips on the down,
And the wet-wood smoke drives us winking blind.
But there's smoke and wind and woe in the town
Harder to bear
There than here,
On the saddest day of the weariest year.

THE SONG OF THE WOMEN: A WEALDEN TRIO[1]

1st Voice:
When ye've got a child 'at's whist for want of food,
And a grate as grey 's y'r 'air for want of wood,
And y'r man and you ain't nowise not much good;

---

[1] Set by Benjamin Britten as 'A Wealden Trio: Christmas Song of the
Women' for unaccompanied voices (London: Faber and Faber, 1968).

Together:

Oh –
It's hard work a-Christmassing,
Carolling,
Singin' songs about the 'Babe what's born.'

2nd Voice:

When ye've 'eered the bailiff's 'and upon the latch,
And ye've felt the rain a-trickling through the thatch,
An' y'r man can't git no stones to break ner yit no sheep to watch –

Together:

Oh –
We've got to come a-Christmassing,
Carolling,
Singin' of the 'Shepherds on that morn.'

3rd Voice, more cheerfully:

'E was a man 's poor as us, very near,
An' 'E 'ad 'is trials and danger,
An' I think 'E 'll think of us when 'E sees us singing 'ere;
For 'is mother was poor, like us, poor dear,
An' she bore him in a manger.

Together:

Oh –
It 's warm in the heavens, but it 's cold upon the earth;
An' we ain't no food at table nor no fire upon the hearth;
And it's bitter hard a-Christmassing,
Carolling,
Singin' songs about our Saviour's birth;
Singin' songs about the Babe what's born;
Singin' of the shepherds on that morn.

THE PEASANT'S APOLOGY

Down near the earth
On the steaming furrows
Things are harsh and black enough
Dearth there is and lack enough,
And immemorial sorrows
Stultify sweet mirth
Till she borrows
Bitterness and blackness from the earth.

A BALLAD OF AN AUCTION
[AUCTIONEER'S SONG]

'At the present moment there is not a tenant farmer working the land between
L— and H— Street – a stretch of ten miles or so. The stock and household
goods of the last of them, a man of sixty-five, sober and industrious, were sold
"by order of the trustees in bankruptcy" at almost nominal prices. The man has
nothing before him but the workhouse.' – *Evidence given before the Royal
Commission on Agriculture*

Come up from the field, come up from the fold,
For the farmer has broken; his things must be sold.
Drive the flock from the fold and the stock from the field,
And the team from the ploughing, and see what they yield.
Come up!

Come up from the marsh, come up from the hops,
Come down from the ventways, and down through the copse,
Come up from the hops, come up from the marsh;
For selling is bitter and creditors harsh.

Bring all you can find, take the clock from the wall,
The crocks from the dairy, the armchair and all.
Tear the prints from the wall, bring all you can find,
Now turn up your collars, to keep out the wind.

So come up from the field, come up from the fold,
For the poor old farmer, his things must be sold,
And come up from the fold, come up from the field,
And we'll stand here together, and see what they yield.
Come up!

'Al'ington Knoll it stands up high
Guidin' the sailors sailin' by
Stands up high for all to see,
Cater the marsh and crost the sea.

'Al'ington Knoll, when we was cubs,
Use 'ter mark where we'd sunk the tubs:
Get it in line with Romney Church,
They revenue chaps was left in the lurch.

'Al'ington Knoll's a mound a-top,
With a dyke all round – an' it's bound to stop:
For them as made it in them ol' days
Sees to it well that theer it stays.

'Farmer Finn as farmed the ground,
Tried to level the goodly mound;
But not a chap from Lydd to Lym'
Thought *that* job was meant for him.

'For that ol' Knoll is watched so well
By drownded men kep' outen hell.
They guards it well an' keeps it whole
For a sailor's mark, the goodly knoll.

'Finn he fetched a chap from the sheeres,
One of yer spunky devil-may-keeres;
Give him a shovel and pick and spade;
Promised him double what we was paid.

'He digged till ten and he muddled on
Till he'd digged up a sword and a skilliton –
A grit old sword as big as me,
An' grit old bones as you could see.

'He digged and digged the livelong day
Till th' sun went down in Fairlight Bay.
He digged and digged, an' behind his back
The lights shone up and the marsh went black.

'An' the sky all round went black from red,
An' the wood went black – *an' the man was dead.*
But where he'd digged the chark shone white
Out to sea like Calais light.

'Al'ington Knoll it stands up high,
Guidin' the sailors a-sailin' by;
Stands up high for all to see,
Cater the marsh and crost the sea.'

A PAGAN

Bright white clouds and April skies
    May make your heart feel bonny,
But summer's sun and flower's growth
    Will fill my hives with honey,
And mead is sweet to a pugging tooth
When it's dark at four and snow clouds rise.

Owl light's sweet if the moon be bright,
    And trysting's no bad folly,
But give me mead and a warm hearth-stone,
    And a cosy pipe and Dolly
– And Dolly to devil a mutton bone
When it's dark at four of a winter's night.

THE PEDLAR LEAVES THE BAR PARLOUR AT DYMCHURCH

Good-night, we'd best be jogging on,
The moon's been up a while,
We've got to get to Bonnington,
Nigh seven mile.

But the marsh ain'd so lone if you've heered a good song,
And you hum it aloud as you cater along,
Nor the stiles half so high, nor the pack so like lead,
If you've heered a good tale an' it runs in your head.

So, come, we'd best be jogging on,
The moon will give us light,
We've got to get to Bonnington
To sleep to-night.

'DU BIST DIE RUH'*

You are to me what other men call 'rest,'
You are to me what other men call 'life's behest,'
Soft are your eyes and cool, and soft and cool are your fingers,
And sweeter, far sweeter, your silence than voice of the sweetest of singers;
And the calmness which comes with your presence clings and lingers
In the hollow of your breast,
My rest.

AN ANNIVERSARY*

Two decades and a minute
And half a moon in the sky,
Like a broken willow pattern plate
And a jangling bell to din it.
Dingle – dong – twelve strokes –
Two decades and a minute.

TANDARADEI

(Walter von der Vogelweide)

Under the lindens on the heather,
There was our double resting-place,
Side by side and close together
Garnered blossoms, crushed, and grass
Nigh a shaw in such a vale,
Tandaradei,
Sweetly sang the nightingale.

I came a-walking through the grasses;
Lo! my dear was come before.
Ah – what befell then – listen – listen, lasses,
Makes me glad for evermore,
Kisses? – thousands in good sooth,
Tandaradei,
See how red they've left my mouth.

There had he made ready – featly, fairly,
All of flow'ring herbs a yielding bed,
And that place in secret still smiles rarely.
If by chance your foot that path should tread,
You might see the roses pressed,
Tandaradei,
Where e'enow my head did rest.

How he lay beside me, did a soul discover,
(Now may God forfend such shame from me),
Not a soul shall know it save my lover,
Not a soul could see save I and he,
And a certain small brown bird,
Tandaradei,
Trust him not to breathe a word.

SONG OF THE HEBREW SEER

Oh would that the darkness would cover the face of the land,
Oh would that a cloud would shroud the face of high heaven,
Would blot out the stars, and hush, hush, hush the winds of the west,
That the sons of men might sink into utter rest,
Forgetting the God in whose name their fathers had striven,
Might strive no longer and slumber as slumbers the desert sand.

That then, oh, my God, should Thy lightnings flash forth,
That Thy voice, oh, Jehovah, should burst on mine ear
In the thunder that rolls from the east and the north
And Thy laugh on the rushing of winds that bear
The myriad, myriad sounds of the sea.

SONNET

(Suggested by the 'Phoebus with Admetus'
by George Meredith)

After Apollo left Admetus' gate,
Did his late fellows feel a numb despair,
Did they cry 'Comrade, comrade' ev'rywhere
Thro' the abandoned byres, and curse the fate
That let them for awhile know him for mate
To mourn his going? Did his vacant chair
Before the fire, when winter drove them there,
Make the sad silence more disconsolate?

Did yearning ears all vainly, vainly strain
To half recall the voice that now was mute?
Did yearning eyes strive all in vain, in vain,
To half recall the glory of his face,
To half recall the God that for a space
Had quickened their dead world? and, ah, his lute . . .

FOR THE BOOKPLATE OF A MARRIED COUPLE*

A book our eyes have glanced on
Together,
A wind that ev'ry feather
And windlestraw hath danced on,

A path our feet have trodden
Together
In still or windy weather,
On springy turf or sodden.

16   *Selected Poems*

IN THE SICK ROOM‡

Beloved: now you're sad and ill
(You must not, must not droop your head)
It makes the whole house still and dead
It makes the whole world sad and still,
Sad, sad and still.

Beloved: rain has thawed the snow
The garden seems to crave your tread
(You must not, must not hang your head)
It makes the night hours sad and slow
Sad, sad and slow.

Beloved: roads are clear: arise:
The field paths wind across the grass
The buds will quicken as you pass
(You must not, must not droop your eyes
Sweet, sweet your eyes).

[A SEQUENCE]

I *Lavender*
You make me think of lavender,
And that is why I love you so;
Your sloping shoulders, heavy hair,
And long swan's neck like snow,
Befit those gracious girls of long ago,
Who in closed gardens took the quiet air;
Who lived the ordered life to gently pass
From earth as from rose petals perfumes go,
Or shadows from that dial in the grass;
Whose fingers from the painted spinet keys
Drew small heart-clutching melodies.
        One may not say
Whether they were more fair,
Or more to be desired than maids to-day.
        I only know
You make me think of lavender,
And that is why I love you so.

II
        I do not ask so much,
– O, bright-hued; oh, tender-eyed –
As you should sometimes shimmer at my side,
                Oh, Fair.

        I do not crave a touch,
Nor, at your comings hither,
Sound of soft laughter, savour of your hair,
Sight of your face; oh fair, oh full of grace,
                I ask not, I.

        But that you do not die,
Nor fade, oh bright, nor wither,
That somewhere in the world your sweet, dim face
Be, unattainable, unpaled by fears,
                Unvisited by years,
                Stained by no tears.

III *Silverpoint*

Come in the delicate stillness of dawn,
    Your eyelids heavy with sleep,
When the faint moon slips to its line dim-drawn,
Grey and a shadow, the sea. And deep, very deep,
    The tremulous stillness ere day in the dawn.

Come, scarce stirring the dew on the lawn,
    Your face still shadowed by dreams,
When the world's all shadow, and rabbit and fawn,
Those timorous creatures of shadows and gleams,
And twilight and dew-light, still people the lawn.

Come, more real than life is real,
    Your form half-seen in the dawn,
A warmth half-felt, like the rays that steal
Hardly revealed from the east; oh warmth of my breast,
O life of my heart, oh intimate solace of me. . . .
So, when the landward breeze steals up from the quickening sea
And the leaves quiver of a sudden, and life is here and the day,
    You shall fade away and pass
As – when we breathed upon your mirror's glass –
    Our faces died away.

IV *The Small Philosophy*[1]
      C'est toi qui dors dans l'ombre, ô sacré souvenir

If we could have remembrance now
And see, as in the winter's snow
We shall, what's golden in these hours,
The flitting, swift, intangible desires of sea and strand!

Who sees what's golden where we stand?
The sky's too bright, the sapphire sea too green;
I, I am fevered, you cold-sweet, serene,
And . . . and . . .

---

[1] A revised version of this poem (without the title) was used as the epigraph
for the major collaborative novel Ford wrote with Conrad, *Romance* (1903).

Yet looking back in days of snow
Unto this olden day that's now,
We'll see all golden in these hours
This memory of ours.

V

It was the Autumn season of the year
When ev'ry little bird doth ask his mate:
'I wonder if the Spring will find us here,
It groweth late.'

I saw two Lovers walking through the grass,
And the sad He unto his weeping Dear
Did say: 'Alas!
When Spring comes round I shall no more be here,
For I must sail across the weary sea
And leave the waves a-churn 'twixt you and me.

'Oh, blessed Autumn! blest late Autumn-tide!
For ever with thy mists us Lovers hide.
Ignore Time's laws
And leave thy scarlet haws
For ever on the dewy-dripping shaws
Of this hillside.
Until the last, despite of Time and Tide,
Give leave that we may wander in thy mist,
With the last, dread
Word left for aye unsaid
And the last kiss unkisst.'

It was the Autumn season of the year,
When ev'ry little bird doth ask his mate:
'I wonder if the Spring will find us here,
It groweth late.'

VI *To a Tudor Tune*

When all the little hills are hid in snow,
And all the small brown birds by frost are slain,
And sad and slow the silly sheep do go,
All seeking shelter to and fro,
Come once again,
To these familiar, silent, misty lands,
Unlatch the lockless door,
And cross the drifted floor,
Ignite the waiting, ever-willing brands,
And warm thy frozen hands,
By the old flame once more.
Ah, heart's desire, once more by the old fire, stretch out thy hands.

A GREAT VIEW [THE GREAT VIEW]

Up here where the air's very clear
And the hills slope away nigh down to the bay
It is very like Heaven. . . .
For the sea's wine-purple and lies half asleep
In the sickle of the shore and serene in the West,
Lion-like, purple, and brooding in the even,
Low hills lure the sun to rest.

Very like Heaven . . . For the vast marsh dozes,
And waving plough-lands and willowy closes
Creep and creep up the soft south steep.
In the pallid North the grey and ghostly downs do fold away,
And, spinning spider threadlets down the sea, the sea-lights dance
And shake out a wavering radiance.

Very like Heaven . . . For a shimmering of pink,
East, far east, past the sea-lights' distant blink,
Like a cloud shell-pink, like the ear of a girl,
Like Venice-glass mirroring mother-o'-pearl,
Like the small pink nails of my lady's fingers,
Where the skies drink the sea and the last light lies and lingers . . .
        There is France!

ON THE HILLS

> Keep your brooding sorrows for dewy-misty hollows.
> Here's your blue sky and lark song, drink the air. The joy that follows
> Drafts of wine o' west wind, o' north wind, o' summer breeze,
> Never grape's hath equalled from the wine hills by the summer seas.
> Whilst the breezes live, joy shall contrive,
> Still to tear asunder, and to scatter near and far
> Those nets small and thin
> That spider sorrows spin
> In the brooding hollows where no breezes are.

SIDERA CADENTIA
(ON THE DEATH OF QUEEN VICTORIA)

When one of the old, little stars doth fall from its place,
The eye,
Glimpsing aloft must sadden to see that its space
        In the sky
Is darker, lacking a spot of its ancient, shimmering grace,
And sadder, a little, for loss of the glimmer on high.

Very remote, a glitter, a mote far away, is your star,
But its glint being gone from the place where it shone
The night's somewhat grimmer and something is gone
Out of the comforting quiet of things as they are.

        A shock
A change in the beat of the clock;
And the ultimate change that we fear feels a little less far.

A NIGHT PIECE [NIGHT PIECE]

But, of those better tides of dark and melancholy,
When one's abroad in a field, the night very deep, very holy,
The turf very sodden a-foot, walking heavy, the small ring of light,
Of the lanthorn one carries, a-swinging to left and to right,
Revealing a flicker of hedge-row, a flicker of rushes – and night
Ev'rywhere; ev'rywhere sleep and a hushing to sleep –
I know that I never shall utter the uttermost secrets aright,
They lie so deep.

GREY MATTER

She. They leave us nothing.
He.   Still, a little's left.
She. A crabbèd, ancient, dried biologist,
Somewhere very far from the sea, closed up from the sky,
Shut in from the leaves, destroys our hopes and us.
He. Why, no, our hopes and . . .
She.   In his 'Erster Heft,'
Page something, I forget the line, he says
That, hidden as deep in the brain as he himself from hope,
There's this grey matter.
He.   Why, 'tis there, dear heart.
She. That, if that hidden matter cools, decays,
Dies – what you will – our souls die out as well;
Since, hidden in the millionth of a cell,
Is all we have to give us consciousness.
He. Suppose it true.
She.   Ah, never; better die,
Better have never lived than face this mist,
Better have never toiled to such distress.
He. It matters little.
She.   Little! Where shall I,
The woman, where shall you take part,
My poet? Where has either of us scope
In this dead-dawning century that lacks all faith,
All hope, all aim, and all the mystery
That comforteth. Since he victorious

With his cold vapours chills out you and me,
The woman and the poet?
He.   Never, dear.
For you and I remain,
The woman and the poet. And soft rain
Still falls and still the crocus flames,
The blackbird calls.
She.   But half the sweet is gone.
The voices of our children at their games
Lack half their ring.
He.   Why, never, dear. Out there,
The sea's a cord of silver, still to south
Beyond the marsh.
She.   Ah, but beyond it all,
And all beneath and all above, half of the glory's done.
And I and you. . . .
He.   Why, no. The ancient sun
Shines as it ever shone, and still your mouth
Is sweet as of old it was.
She.   But what remains?
He. All the old pains,
And all the old sweet pleasures and the mystery
Of time, slow travel and unfathomed deep.
She. And then this cold extinction? . . .
He.   Dreamless sleep.
She. And nothing matters?
He.   All the old, old things.
        Whether to Church or College rings
            The clamorous bell of creeds,
                We, in the lush, far meads.
Poet and woman, past the city walls,
Hear turn by turn the burden of their calls,
Believe what we believe, feel what we feel,
Like what we list of what they cry within
        Cathedral or laborat'ry,
Since, by the revolution of the wheel,
The one swings under, let us wait content.
She. Yet it is hard.
He.   Ah, no. A sure intent,
        For me and you.
The right, true, joyful word, the sweet, true phrase,
The calling of our children from the woods these garden days

Remain. – These drops of rain have laid the dust
And in our soft brown seed-beds formed the crust
We needed for our sowings. Bring your seed,
And you shall prick it in, I close the row.
Be sure the little grains your hands have pressed
Tenderly, lovingly, home, shall flourish best.
She. Aye, you are still my poet.
He.   Even so
Betwixt the rain and shine. Half true's still true
More truly than the thing that's proved and dead.
The sun lends flame to every crocus head
Once more, and we once more must sow and weed
Since in the earth the newly stirring seed
Begins the ancient mystery anew.

FROM THE SOIL: [TWO MONOLOGUES]

The Field Labourer speaks.

Ah am a mighty simple man and only
Good wi' my baggin' hook and sichlike and 'tis lonely
Wheer Ah do hedge on Farmer Finn his farm.
            Often Ah gits to thinking
When it grows dark and the ol' sun's done sinking,
And Ah hev had my sheere
            Of fear
And wanted to feel sure that God were near
            And goodly warm –
As near as th'eldritch shave I were at wark about . . .
            Plenty o' time for thinking
We hes between the getting up and sinking
Of that ol' sun – about the God we tark about . . .
    .   .   .   .

In the beginning God made Heaven and
The 'Arth, 'n Sea we sometimes hear a-calling
When wind she bloweth from the rainy land
An' says ther'll soon be wet an' rain a-falling.

Ah'll give you, parson, God He made the sea,
An' made this 'Arth, ner yit Ah wo-an't scrimmage
But what He made the sky; what passes *me*
Is that what follows: 'Then the Lord made we
      In his own image.'

For, let alone the difference in us creatures,
Some short o' words like me, and others preachers
With stores of them, like you; some fair, some middlin',
Some black-avis'd like you and good at fiddlin',
Some crabb'd, some mad, some mighty gay and pleasant,
No two that's more alike than jackdaw is to pheasant,
        We're poorish stuff at best.

We doesn't last no time before we die,
Nor leave more truck behind than they poor thrushes.
You find, stiff feathers, laid aside the bushes
After a hard ol' frost in Janu-ry
    Ol' crow he lives much longer,
    Ol' mare's a de-al stronger
      'N the hare's faster . . .
If so be God's like we and we like He
      The man's as good's his Master.

You are a civil, decent spoken man, Muss Parson
'N' *I* don't think ye'll say this kind o' tark is worse 'n arson –
That's burning stacks, I think – sure*ly* it isn' meant so
    I tell you, Parson, no;
'N' us poor folk we doesn't want to blame
You parsons fer the things that's said and sung
Up there in church. My apple tree is crook'd because twere bent so
When it were young.
'N' them as had you preacher-folk to tame,
Taught you the tales that you are bound to tell
    Us folk below
About three Gods that's one an' Heav'n an' Hell,
An' things us folk ain't *meant* to understand.

I tell you, sir, we men that's on the land
Needs summut we can chew when trouble's brewing,
When our ol' 'ooman's bad an' rent is due
      'N' we no farden,

'N' when it's late to sow 'n' still too wet to dig the garden,
Something as we can chew like that ol' cow be chewing.
Something told plain and something we gits holt on,
– You need a simple sort o' feed to raise a colt on –
We needs it, parson, life's a bitter scrimmage,
Livin' and stuggin' in the mud and things we do
        Enow confound us;
We hain't no need for fear
Of God, to make the living hardly worth . . .

You tell us, sir, that 'God He made this Earth
        In His own image'
An' make the Lord seem near.
So's we could think that when we come to die
        We'll lie
In this same goodly 'Arth, an' things goo on around us
        Much as they used to goo.

II   *The Small Farmer soliloquizes*

I wonder why we toiled upon the earth
From sunrise until sunset, dug and delved,
Crook-backed, cramp-fingered, making little marks
On the unmoving bosoms of the hills,
And nothing came of it. And other men
In the same places dug and delved and ended
As we have done; and other men just there
Shall do the self-same things until the end.
I wonder why we did it. . . . Underneath
The grass that fed my sheep, I often thought
Something lay hidden, some sinister thing
Lay looking up at us as if it looked
Upwards thro' quiet waters; that it saw
Us futile toilers scratching little lines
And doing nothing. And maybe it smiled
Because it knew that we must come to this. . . .

I lay and heard the rain upon the roof
All night when rain spelt ruin, lay and heard
The east wind shake the windows when that wind
Meant parched up land, dried herbage, blighted wheat,

The Face Of The Night 27

And ruin, always ruin creeping near
In the long droughts and bitter frosts and floods.
And when at dawning I went out-a-doors
I used to see the top of the tall shaft
O' the workhouse here, peep just above the downs,
It was as if the thing were spying, waiting,
Watching my movements, saying, 'You will come,
Will come at last to me.' And I am here . . .
And down below that Thing lay there and smiled;
Or no, it did not smile; it was as if
One might have caught it smiling, but one saw
The earth immovable, the unmoved sheep
And senseless hedges run like little strings
All over hill and dale. . . .

TO CHRISTINA AT NIGHTFALL

Little thing, ah, little mouse,
Creeping through the twilit house,
To watch within the shadow of my chair
With large blue eyes; the firelight on your hair
Doth glimmer gold and faint,
And on your woollen gown
That folds a-down
From steadfast little face to square-set feet.

Ah, sweet! ah, little one! so like a carven saint,
With your unflinching eyes, unflinching face,
Like a small angel, carved in a high place,
Watching unmoved across a gabled town;
When I am weak and old,
And lose my grip, and crave my small reward
Of tolerance and tenderness and ruth,
The children of your dawning day shall hold
The reins we drop and wield the judge's sword
And your swift feet shall tread upon my heels,
And I be Ancient Error, you New Truth,
And I be crushed by your advancing wheels. . . . . .

Good-night! The fire is burning low,
Put out the lamp;
Lay down the weary little head
Upon the small white bed.
Up from the sea the night winds blow
Across the hill across the marsh;
Chill and harsh, harsh and damp,
The night winds blow.
But, while the slow hours go,
I, who must fall before you, late shall wait and keep
Watch and ward,
Vigil and guard,
Where you sleep.
Ah, sweet! do you the like where I lie dead.

WIFE TO HUSBAND

If I went past you down this hill,
And you had never seen my face before,
Would all your being feel the sudden thrill
You said it felt, once more?

If I went past you through this shaw,
Would you be all a-quiver at the brush
Of my trailed garments; would the sudden hush
You said the black-birds' voices had in awe
Of my first coming, fall upon the place
Once more, if you had never seen my face
Nor ever heard my passing by before,
And nought had passed of all that was of yore?

TWO FRESCOES

It occurred to me that a series of frescoes might arise dealing with the fortunes of Roderick the Goth. Having neither wall nor brushes I have tried to put two of them upon paper.

I   *The Tower*

Down there where Europe's arms
Stretch out to Africa,
Throughout the storms, throughout the calms
Of centuries it took the alms
Of sun and rain; the loud alarms
Of war left it unmoved; and grey
And brooding there it watched the strip of foam
And fret of ruffled waters, was the home
Of the blue rock-dove and the birds o' the main.

Coming from Africa
The swallows rested on it flying north
In spring-time; rested there again,
When the days shorten, speeding on the way
Homewards to Africa
Back and forth
The tiny ships below sped; east and west
It was called blest
By mariners it guided. Mystery
Hung round it like a veil. The ancient Ones,
They said, had seen it rise
Upwards to the old suns,
Upwards to the old skies,
When Hercules
Did bid it guard those seas.

It was a thing of the Past;
Stood there untroubled; like a virgin, dreamed;
And not a man of all that land but deemed
The tower sacred.
It was a symbol of an ancient faith,
Some half-forgotten righteousness, some Truth,
Some virtue in the land whose tillers said:
'Whilst that stands unenforced, it is well.'
Be sure the thing is even so to-day,
Our tower doth somewhere unenforced rise

Upwards to our old skies.
And if we suffer sacrilegious hands
To force its innocence, our knell shall ring
As it rang out for them on that old day
Knolling from Africa.
You say it was the King who did this thing,
Who sinned against this righteousness. But say:
If we stand by and with averted eyes,
Or, shrugging shoulders, let our rulers sin
Against the very virtue of the race,
Who is it then but us must bear the pains
Of Nemesis? Ah, yes, it was the King. . . .

II   *Goths*

'Let the stars flame by as the flaming earth falls down,
Ruined fall the earth as the clanging heavens fall.
Clasp me, love of mine; be the jewels in my crown
But the firelit tears of Gods, of the Ancient Ones of all.'

The swart King paced his palace wall
And down below the maids at ball
Sang in choir at evenfall
As they played:

'Make our couch of Greece and the footstool for our throne
        Of Rome, throw scented Spain for the incense of our fire,
Bring me all the East for the jewels in my zone
        Cast them all together for our leaping wedding pyre.'

And he looked down
Into their cloistral shade
And saw, without the tongues of shadow thrown
By wall and tree of that sequestered place
One girl who had the sunlight on her face,
Who swayed and clapped her hands and sang alone.

'My father can but die,' she sang,
'My mother can but weep,
This weary town fall blazing down
And be a smouldering heap
Beneath the flame

Where I was wont to keep
My weary vigil till my lover came.'

Chanting in her pauses all the girls within the close
Sang to her singing, and their hidden chorus rose
Like a wave, fell like falling asleep.
And for the King, her voice like fiery wine
Set all his pulses throbbing and her face
Did dazzle more than did the blood-red sun.

'He who would win me, let him woo like this,
Flames on his face and the blood upon his hands,
Ravish me away when the blackening embers hiss
As the red flesh weeps to the brands.'

That King was one who reignèd there alone
Upon those very confines of the world,
Where conquering races ebb to sloth and sink
As still great rivers sink into the sands.
And – for his fathers had been rav'ning wolves
Who coursed through ruin, pestilence and death
When all the world flamed red from end to end –
That ancient song of his destroying race
The girl sang stirred the fibres of his frame
Till all the earth was red before his face.
It had been so the women sang of old
To his forgotten sires, and still they sang
Within the shadow of his palace wall,
The cloister of his grimmest liege of all.
And as she sang the ferment worked in her
And shook her virgin's voice to jarring notes.
Stirring in her the ancient cry of throats
Torn with the passions of the ancient days.

'Pour me blood o' gods; bring me broken oaths for toys
Countless of the cost, of their ruin, of thine own;
Drunk with wine and passion, drink thy moment's fill of joys,
Godlike, beastlike, manlike, drink and cast thy cup a-down;
    Lose thy life; give thy crown,
    Lose thy soul, give thine all,
As we sink to death and ruin with the smoke o' worlds for pall.'

And so she raised her eyes and saw the King
Stand frowning down, his face inspired with flame
Fro' the west'ring sun. And then the Angelus
Chimed out across the silent land of Spain.
Beyond the strip of foam the imaums called,
And Africa and Europe fell to prayer.
But those two gazing in each other's eyes
Looked back into the hollows of the years.
And as he stood above his brooding land
It was as if she saw her sires again.
Flames shone upon his face and on his hands
Incarnadined; whenas the sun sank down
He raised his eyes and seemed to see that Spain
Was all on fire with blood upon the roofs.
And down to South the inviolate, pallid tower
Rose silent, pointing to the crescent moon
And that great peering planet called Sohéil,
That heralds, as Mahomet's doctors say,
His domination and his children's sway,
Rose over Africa.

VOLKSWEISE

A poor girl sat by a tower of the sea
All a-wringing of her hands; 'Will he never show,' says she,
'Just as a token, just a glimmer of his ship's lant . . . horn?'

'Oh, all ye little grains of sand
Twist into a rope shall draw his keel
Hither. Oh, ye little gulls and terns,
Join wings and bear me from this strand
To where I'll feel
His arms, and find where on the foam his ship is borne.'

A poor girl sat, etc.

'Oh, all ye little stars o' the night
Come down and cluster in my hair;
Oh, bright night-flashes o' the waves

Shine round me till I'm all one flame of light.
So, far at sea,
He'll deem a beacon beckons him to me. . . . '

A poor girl sat nigh a tower of the sea
All a-wringing of her hands: 'Will he never show,' said she,
'Just a token, just a glimmer of his ship's lant . . . horn?'

AND AFTERWARDS
(A SAVAGE SORT OF SONG ON THE ROAD)

> *Once I was a gallant and bold I*
> *And you so tender and true,*
> *But I'll never again be the old I*
> *Nor you the old you.*

I shall go lounging along on the edge
Of the grass. . . . You'll loiter along by the hedge.
I shall go dogged through dust and the dirt
Like an ass in my moods.
You with a new sweetheart at your skirt
Ev'ry few roods. . . .

> *'Once I was a gallant,' etc.*

We'll maybe jog along together
A long way;
Maybe put up with the weather together,
Better or worse
As it chances day by day,
Or maybe part with a kick and a curse
I and you,
After a turning or two. . . .

> *'But I'll never again,' etc.*

ON A MARSH ROAD:
(WINTER NIGHTFALL)

A bluff of cliff, purple against the south,
And nigh one shoulder-top an orange pane.
This wet, clean road; clear twilight held in the pools,
And ragged thorns, ghost reeds and dim, dead willows.

Past all the windings of these grey, forgotten valleys,
To west, past clouds that close on one dim rift –
The golden plains; the infinite, glimpsing distances,
The eternal silences; dim lands of peace.

Infinite plains to know no wanderer's foot; infinite
        distances where alone is rest;
All-virgin downs where none shall pasture sheep;
        inviolable peaks that none shall climb,
From whose summit nor you nor I shall gaze on oceans infinite beyond,
Nor none look back upon this world folding to-night, to rain and to sleep.

AT THE END OF A PHASE
[AN END PIECE]

        Close the book,
        And here's an end of ev'rything;
        Pass up from the shore,
        And pass by byre and stall.
For the smacks shall trail home on the tail of the tides,
And the kine still stay deep in the sweet-water sides,
And they still shall be burying, still wedding brides;
        But I must be gone in the morning.

        One more look,
        And then farewell sweet summering;
        A moment more,
        And then no more at all.
For the skipper shall summon his hands to the sea,
And the shepherd still shepherd his sheep on the lea,
But it's over and done with the man that was me,
        And over the hill comes the morning.

FROM INLAND

I dreamed that you and I were young
Once more, and by our old grey sea
Stood in the wind; but matins, sung
High in these wine-hills, wakened me.
I lay, half roused and seemed to hold
Once more beside our old, dear sea,
Your hand. I saw the primrose gold
Your hair had then and seemed to see
Your eyes, so child-like and so wise
Look down on me.

By the last fire we ever lit
You knelt and bending down your head,
– if you could compass it – you said,
Not ever would you live again
Your vanished life, never again
Pass through those shadowy vales of pain.

'And now I'm old and here I sit,'
You said and held your hands apart
To those old flames we've left behind
As far – as far as some dead wind.
And so I fetched from near my heart
Brave platitudes. For you were there
The firelight lit your brooding face
And flickered in your dream-gold hair,
– I could be brave for the short space
I had you near my chair.
As thus: 'Since with the ebb of youth
Rises the flood of passionless
And calm enjoyment, out shines Truth
And fades the painful earnestness
Of all young thought, we two,' I said,
'Have still the best to come.' But you
Bowed still your patient, silent head
                    . . . This view!
Steep vineyards rising parched and brown
This weary stream: this weary town:
White convents on each hill-top! . . .
                    Dear

What would I give to climb our down
Where fresh wind hisses in each stalk,
And from the high brown crest to see
Beyond our ancient sea-grey town
The sky-line of our foam-flecked sea.
Ah, by a sheltered hedge to rest
And looking out to sea to hear,
Ah dear, once more your pleasant talk,
And to go home as twilight falls
Along the old marsh walls. . . .
'The best to come!' The best! The best!
One says the wildest things at times,
Merely for comfort. But – 'The best!'
Ah well . . . At night when the moon climbs,
High o'er these misty inland capes,
And hears the river lisping rhymes,
And sees the roe-deer nibbling grapes,
Amid the evanescent gleams
Of falling dew-drops, shall come dreams
Gliding among the mists beneath,
Maybe a dream of you and me
Young once again by our old sea:

But, ah, we two must travel wide
And far and far ere we shall find
That recollected, ancient tide
We walked by once, or that dead wind
That fled so bravely to its death.

THE PORTRAIT

She sits upon a tombstone in the shade,
One flake of sunlight falls between the leaves
Of quivering poplars, lights upon her hair,
Shot golden, and across her candid brow:
So, in this pleasant gloom she holds the eye:
Being life amid piled up remembrancers
Of the tranquil dead.
                    One hand, dropped lightly down,

Rests on the words of a forgotten name:
And so the past is glad to stay her up
Because her light and life attract the glance
In pity to this resting-place no foot
Has sought these many hours . . .
                              So many hours!
'Tis a forgotten place, closed in, walled off,
Deep, planted in with yews, unvisited,
A still backwater in the tide of life.
Sounds from surrounding streets, rising to heaven,
Just penetrate its silence: footfalls, cries,
Laughter of children and the roll of wheels.
And she sits waiting: light and the shade,
A flame in a dim underworld half seen.
There's a small smile, you see, around her lips,
And tiny sparks of light swim in her eyes
Because she sits and waits and one shall come
To this soft summer coolness. – Love shall come
That holdeth back the past and doth hand down
The life of all the world to times unborn.
So she rejoices us who pass her by,
And she rejoices those who here lie still,
And she makes glad the little wandering airs,
And lends a lustre to the shafts of light
That fall upon her face; and all the world
Moves round her as she sits upon her tomb
And waits her traveller's coming.
                              She is Life:
The secret of the Universe: the prize
That makes us keep to toiling: travelling roads,
Hauling our burdens up the unending hill,
Pondering senseless problems, setting sail
For undiscovered lands. She is the end:
She waits, she waits, sequestered, among tombs,
The sunlight in her hair. She waits, she waits:
Offering rest: she, the resolving note
That puts in tune all this discordant world
And solves the riddles of delight and pain.

TWO MAKING MUSIC*

These are her songs: tho' his voice lifted be,
And his hand wrote the words and set the key,
She, listening, is voiced in what she hears:
Here are her very form and melody
Now rendered back to her beloved ears.

She plays on him as on an instrument,
And all his notes, resounding to her touch,
Do give her forth into the twilight room.
Here is her voice: it soundeth but of her;
Here are her words: they tell of her alone;
And here her penmanship: she guides his hand;
Here are her face and presence: he sees naught
But her in all the world, and he is naught
But, as it were, a harp set quivering
By memories of her that pass and pass
Like little winds fretting the sounding string
Stretched in dim arbours o'er the twilight grass.

These are her songs: it is not he doth sing,
But she herself hymning herself. Alas!
Here we have perfect beauty mirroring
Itself in a cracked glass.

SONG

Oh, purer than the day new-born,
More candid than the pearlèd morn,
Come soon and set the day in tune
All thro' the sun-bathed afternoon,
Come soon!

Oh, sweeter than the roses be,
Subtler than balm or rosemary,
Come now, and 'neath this orchard bough
Set your cool lips to my hot brow,
Come now!

More rhythmic when you sleep than tunes
Waft o'er the waves in summer moons,
Stay here, and in my longing ear
Murmur the words I crave to hear,
Rest here!

Here, in the shadowy sacred place,
Close up your eyes, hide your dear face,
And in these shadows sink to rest.
Now the cool night falls; dear and blest,
Now sleep, a dim and dreamless sleep,
Whilst I watch over you and keep
Your soul from fears. Now sleep!

Oh, purer than the morning light
And more beloved than dead of night
Come soon to set the world in tune
From midnight till the dial marks noon:
From dawn till the world's end. Come soon!
Come soon!

A SUABIAN LEGEND

I
God made all things,
And seeing they were good
He set a limit to the springs,
And circumscribed the flood,
Stayed the aspiring mountain ranges,
And said: 'Thus far: henceforth no changes.'
And then 'twixt beast and beast he set his ban,
And drew his line 'twixt woman and 'twixt man.

II
God leaning down
Over the world beneath,
Knitted his brows to a frown . . .
No creature drew its breath,

No cloud approached with rain unto the hills;
No ripple moved the mirrors of the seas,
Still lay the cattle in the meads; the rills
Hung in the tufts of moss: the trees
Seemed carven out of metal: manhood stood
Drooping his silent head by womanhood:
No voice of beasts nor any song of bird,
Nor any sound of wind was from the woodlands heard.

III
God leaning down
Over the world beneath,
Knitted his brows to a frown,
And fashioned Death. . . .
The clouds died out around the mountain heads,
The becks and streams sank in their pebbled beds,
The ocean shivered and lay wan, like lead,
And man fled and the beasts fled
Into the crevices of mountains round;
The grass withered on the sod;
Lizards and beetles sank into the ground:
And God
Looked on his last-made creature, Death, and frowned.

IV
He paced in thought a while,
Resounding through his pavèd courts above:
They lightened in the radiance of his smile –
He had imagined Love.
(Oh help us ere we die: we die so soon,
We who have but one dawn and but one noon,
And fade e'er nightfall) . . . Then the Lord made Love.
And looking on the earth he saw
The greenness deepen on each straw:
The worms come creeping on the lawns:
Sweet showers in the pleasant dawns:
The lapwings wailing o'er the fens:
The ewe lambs rising in their pens:
And wavelets tracing rhymes of white
On the blue breast of ocean . . .

                                        But at night
Man slept with woman. Then Creation shook
At the awful wrath of God. His way he took
Over the trembling hills to their embowered nook
Of shadow, where the lime-trees kissed the brook.
Above their sleep he towered: waiting on his word,
Great Death stood by him raising up his sword.
But pausing there above these sleeping things,
God was aware of one whose insubstantial wings,
A-quiver, formed a pent-house o'er the place.
Therefore he stayed his hand and sighed
To see how lip matched lip, side mated side,
And how remembered joy sealed each still face.
Therefore he stayed his hand and smiled,
Shook his tremendous head and went his way,
Love being his best-begotten child
And having over Death and Sin God's sway.
{Oh help us ere we die: we die so soon:
We, who are born at dawn, have but one noon,
And fade ere night: Help us to one short boon,
Help us to know short joy: we die so soon,
So soon: so soon!)

MIDWINTER NIGHT[†]

Now cometh on the dead time of the year:
Meadows in flood and heaths all barren are.
Across the downs and black, tempestuous leas
Blow the dull boomings of deserted seas.
No horsemen fare abroad: no shepherds watch.
And shivering birds cower within the thatch:
But up the wind, around and down the gale
Steeple to steeple, bell to bell doth hail:

'Rest ye: 'tis well.' – Thus in the black o' night
Thro' rainy distance, hid from touch and sight
Man unto man doth make his kinship known
And cries from bell-throats: 'God doth own his own,
Being man!'

Lo, in the warmths and golden lights
Sheltering by hearths, 'neath roofs, thro' these fell nights
Home from the barren heaths and hungry seas
We voyage bravely towards awakening:
Since dead o' the year leads on to distant spring,
Sleep towards daybreak, and old memories
Unto new deeds to do.
                           So bell to bell
Calleth across the folds: *'Rest ye: 'tis well.*
Christ's Man and King: Night's dead, they tell.
Winter hath lost her sting, the Scriptures tell.'

THE PHILOSOPHY OF A LOVER AND GENTLEMAN[†]

A flower, a kiss, a tear – and there's our life.
Long flowers of doubt; short taste of fruit; the knife
Of parting; then the mourning cloths of Death.
That lasts for ever.

This handkerchief I wear against my heart
Once dried a tear of yours. Now it bides here,
And shall till I am summoned to depart. . . .
How odd the things that we find comfort in!
I have picked violets – in that dreary year
When all my life was doubt – picked them because
I had the longing for you in my mind
So powerful, so painful and so sweet, it seemed
Some savour of your presence must pervade
The buds my eyes dwelt on – and so these flowers
Fading to dust within my pocket book.

Now you have kissed me and I have withheld
For a long day my lips from speech and food,
To leave them yours alone till set of sun,
A foolish whim. . . . But you did kiss me. Ah!
What shall enshrine remembrance of a kiss
Or hold its ghost from dawn to set of sun
For me, who have so many hours to live,
Or let my heart recall the mighty throb

That came when you said *'Dear!'* from your deep chest
With wavering fulness?
                            So you shed one tear
Since all was done. Then came the handkerchief . . .
Why, that's the shroud that wraps the Past. That's all
Remains for me to take some comfort in:
This is the catalogue: Some dust of flowers,
A linen cerecloth, and a vanished kiss
And all's summed up. – Save that I live in hell
And have no rest. –
                            But that's another mood
Here we talk gently, being gentlefolk
Without much show of passion, rise of breath,
Quaver of voice, hard eyes, or touch of fever.

A flower, a kiss, a tear – and there's our life.
Long flowers of doubt; short taste of fruit; the knife
Of parting; then the mourning cloths of Death.
That lasts for ever.

VIEWS

I

    Being in Rome I wonder will you go
        Up to the Hill. But I forget the name. . . .
    Aventine? Pincio? No: I do not know.
        I was there yesterday and watched. You came.

The seven Pillars of the Forum stand
High, stained and pale 'neath the Italian heavens,
Their capitals linked up form half a square;
A grove of silver poplars spears the sky.
You came. Do you remember? Yes, you came,
But yesterday. Your dress just brushed the herbs
That nearly hide the broken marble lion. . . .
And I was watching you against the sky.
Such light! Such air! Such prism hues! and Rome
So far below; I hardly knew the place.
The domed St Peter's; mass of the Capitol;
The arch of Trajan and St Angelo. . . .
Tiny and grey and level; tremulous
Beneath a haze amidst a sea of plains. . . .
But I forget the name, who never looked
On any Rome but this of unnamed hills.

II

Tho' you're in Rome you will not go, my You,
        Up to that Hill. . . . but I forget the name,
Aventine? Pincio? No, I never knew. . . .
        I was there yesterday. You never came.

I have that Rome; and you, you have a Me,
You have a Rome and I, I have my You;
Oh passing lonely souls we sons of men!
My Rome is not your Rome: my you, not you
Oh passing lonely. . . . For, if man knew woman
I should have plumbed your heart; if woman, man
Your me should be true I. . . . If in your day –
You who have mingled with my soul in dreams,
You who have given my life an aim and purpose,

A heart, an imaged form – if in your dreams
You have imagined unfamiliar cities
And me among them; I shall never stand
Beneath your pillars or your poplar groves, . . .
Images, simulacra, towns of dreams
That never march upon each other's borders
And bring no comfort to each other's hearts!

III

Nobly accompanied am I! – Since you,
You – simulacrum, image, dream of dreams,
Amidst these images and simulacra
Of shadowy house fronts and these dim, thronged streets
Are my companion!
                    Where the pavements gleam
I have you alway with me: and grey dawns
In the far skies bring you more near – more near
Than City sounds can interpenetrate.
All vapours form a background for your face
In this unreal town of real things,
My you doth stand beside me and make glad
All my imagined cities and doth walk
Beside me towards yet unimagined hills. . . .

Being we two, full surely we shall go
Up to that Hill. . . . some synonym for Home.
Avalon? Grave? or Heaven? I do not know. . . .
But one day or to-day, the day may come,
When I may be your I, your Rome my Rome.

CASTLES IN THE FOG
[FINCHLEY ROAD]

As we come up from Baker Street,
Where Tubes and Trains and 'Buses meet,
There's a touch of frost and a touch of sleet
And mist and mud up Hampstead way
Towards the shutting in of day. . . .

You should be a Queen – or a Duchess rather,
Reigning in place of a warlike father,
In peaceful times, in a tiny town,
With crooked streets all winding down
From your little palace, – a small, old place
Where every soul should know your face,
And love you well – That's what I mean –
A small Grand-Duchess – no distant Queen
Lost in a great land, sitting alone
In a marble palace upon a throne. . . .

– But you'd say to your shipmen: 'Take your ease,
To-morrow is time enough for the seas!'
And prescribe to your bondsmen milder rules
And let the children loose from the schools –
No wrongs for righting, no sores to fester,
In your small Great Hall, 'neath a firelit dais
You'd sit with me at your feet, your jester,
Stroking your shoes where the seed pearls glisten
And talking my nonsense, and you, as your way is,
Would sometimes heed and at times not listen,
But ply your needles and gaze at the brands
And often leave me one of your hands,
Or bid me write you a little ode
Half quaint, half mad, half serious . . .

But here we are at Finchley Road,
With a drizzling rain and a skidding 'bus
And the twilight settling down on us.

JUNE IN TOWN:
1. – THE THREE-TEN AT KILBURN [THE THREE-TEN]

When in the prime and May Day time dead lovers went a-walking,
How bright the grass in lads' eyes was, how easy poet's talking!
Here were green hills and daffodils and copses to contain them:
Daisies for floors did front their doors agog for maids to chain them.
So when the ray of rising day did pierce the eastern heaven
Maids did arise to make the skies seem brighter far by seven.

– Now here's a street where 'bus routes meet and 'twixt the wheels and paving
Standeth a lout that doth hold out flowers not worth the having.
But see, but see! The clock marks three above the Kilburn Station,
Those maids, thank God! are 'neath the sod and all their generation.

What shall she wear who'll soon appear, it is not hood nor wimple,
But by the powers there are no flowers so stately or so simple,
And paper shops and full 'bus tops confront the sun so brightly
That, come three ten, no lovers then had hearts that beat so lightly
As ours, or loved more truly,
Or found green shades or flowered glades to fit their loves more duly.
And see, and see! 'Tis ten past three above the Kilburn Station
Those maids, thank God! are 'neath the sod and all their generation.

2. – FOUR IN THE MORNING COURAGE

The birds this morning wakened me so early it was hardly day:
Ten sparrows in the lilac tree, a blackbird in the may,
A starling somewhere in the mews, a song-thrush on a broken hat
Down in the yard the grocers use, all cried: 'Beware! Beware! The Cat!'
I've never had the heart to rhyme this year: I've always wakened sad
And late, if might be, so the time would be more short – but I was glad
With a mad gladness in to-day that is the longest day in June.
(That blackbird's nesting in the may) For only yesterday at noon
In the long grass of Holland Park, I think – I think – I heard a lark . . . .
I heard your voice: I saw your face once more. . . . *(Upon that packing case*
The starling waked me ere the day aping the thrush's sober tune).

MODERN LOVE

I

Knee-deep among the buttercups, the sun
Gilding the scutcheons and the gilded mail,
Gilding the crowned helm and leopard crest,
Dear, see they pant and strike at your desire.

And one goes down among the emerald grass,
And one stands over him his dagger poised,
His visor raised, his blood-shot eyes a-travel
Over the steel that lies between his feet,
Crushing the buttercups . . . and so the point goes in
Between the gorget and the habergeon . . .
And blood floods out upon the buttercups,
Gules, or and *vert* beneath an azure sky.

And now the victor strides knee-deep in grass,
His surcoat brushing down the flower-heads
To where above the hedge a hennin peeps
Wide, white and waving like a wild swan's wings,
And a green dress, a mantlet all of vair
And such dear eyes. Dear, you've the dearest eyes
In all the world – the most compassionate eyes.

II

. . . In your garden, here
The light streams down between the silvered leaves,
And we sit still and whisper . . . But our fight!
The gross Black Prince among the buttercups
Could grin and girn and pant and sweive and smite
And, in ten minutes it was win or lose:
A coffin board or ale, a coarse caress
Or just an end of it for Life or Death . . .

Is that a footfall on the gravel path?
Are your stretched nerves on edge? And do you see?
There, white and black, the other couple go.
And if some others knew! Oh, buttercups,
And blood upon the grass beneath the sun . . .
Give me your garden where the street lamp shines
Between the leaves: your garden seat, your hand,
Just touching mine – and all the long, long fight
That lies before us, you of the dear eyes.

CONSIDER[1]

Now green comes springing o'er the heath,
And each small bird with lifted breath
Cries 'Brother, consider the joy there is in living!'
'Consider! consider!' the jolly throstle saith.

The golden gorse, the wild thyme frail
And sweet, the butter cowslip pale,
Cry 'Sisters, consider the peace that comes with giving!
And render, and render your sweet and scented breath!'

Now men, come walking o'er the heath
To mark this pretty world beneath,
Bethink them: 'Consider what joy might lie in living,
None striving, constraining none, and thinking not on Death.'

CLUB NIGHT

There was an old man had a broken hat,
He had a crooked leg, an old tame cat,
An old lame horse that cropped along the hedge,
And an old song that set your teeth on edge,
        With words like:

'Club night's come; it's time the dance begins.
Up go the lamps, we've all got nimble shins.
One night a year man and wife may dance at ease
And we'll dance all the village to its knees.'

This silly old man had a broken heart;
He went a-peddling onions from his cart.
Once years ago, when Club night fell in June,
His new-wed wife went off with a dragoon,
        Whilst he sang:

[1] Set to music by 'Peter Warlock' [pseudonym of Philip Heseltine]
(Oxford: Oxford University Press, 1924).

'Club night's come; it's time the dance begins.
Up go the lamps, we've all got nimble shins.
One night a year man and wife may dance at ease
And we'll dance all the village to its knees.'

MAURESQUE
(To V.M.)

To horse! To horse! the veil of night sinks softly down.
The hills are violet, the desert brown,
And thou asleep upon the silken pillows
Within the small white town.

We ride! We ride! and o'er the sand in billows
The crescent moon looks softly down.

A TOAST BEFORE CHANGE [IN THE STONE JUG:
(Tom of Hounslow Heath sings on the night before his execution)]

Ille potens . . . et laetus cui licet in diem Dixisse: Vixi.

Old days are gone,
Here's luck and come better!
Brave suns once shone,
Shall they ne'er rise again?
Here's a queer inn for to-night, but the next one
We will contrive shall be purged of what's vext one
In this; and to-morrow, for all that's perplext one,
I shall awake with a head free of pain.

Here's luck, my friends!
Though to-day's proved my finish,
And this tap now ends,
Shall we ne'er brew again?
Ay, by my faith and the faith I have in you,
You who have kissed and have laughed at the sin – you
Witch that I gambled and squandered to win – you
Too shall come in with me out of the rain.

Old days are gone,
I go to find better;
Brave suns once shone,
They're as good as they were.
I'll cast thy sins in the chops of the Devil:
Old days so brave not the saints dare call evil
In Heaven. Why, if we'd lived cautious and level,
D'ye think I'd have heart to face sunrise up there?

EVERY MAN: A SEQUENCE*

I *The Ploughman*

I am the ruler of all Kings
Who bear the State upon my back;
All wealth comes from my furrowings;
If I should stay my hand what lack,
What dearth and what despair, what death,
Where now waves wheat, what bitter heath!
I plough green lands, by shaws all brown,
Whilst knaves rise up and kings fall down.

II *The Blacksmith*

I am the ruler of all Kings.
This hammer, owning me for lord,
Lo now upon my anvil rings,
And there's your ploughshare, there your sword.
If I should stay my weighty hand
No corn could ripen on the land,
No blade should shield the widow's cause
Nor freeman arm to guard the laws.

III *The Citizen*

I am the ruler of all Kings,
Creator, I, of marts and ports:
All laws I give to present things
And for the future in my Courts.

Lo! Men to be must rest content
To bow before my Parliament,
When I am dead, and own the sway
Of the strong laws I make to-day.

IV *The Preacher*

I am the ruler of all Kings.
Dictator, I, of Faith and Right,
And where my voice saith pleasant things
There shall be comfort in the night.
Before my wrath the People pales
And the embattled fortress fails:
When kings and peoples pass away
I lead them to eternal day.

V *The Poet*

I am the ruler of all Kings,
Creator I of fames to be.
At my command the night-bird sings
Your ancient loves, and, on the sea,
All olden fleets set in array
And golden ages own my sway.
Lo, king or ploughman, dead and gone,
In my loved pages shall live on.

VI *All the Dead*

We are the ruler of all Kings,
We are the Cause who here lie still:
What we once wrought all living things
Helpless endure. – Athwart this hill
Our feet wore pathways Every Man
Must travel on as best he can:
His changeless Past and Cause were we
Who ever were and e'er shall be.

TO GERTRUDE†

It's very late: it's very cold:
And you're too young and I'm too old.
You've your small cares and I've small ease.
Come nestle down across my knees.

Stir up the fire: draw out the chair,
Kick off the shoes: let down the hair:
Your white kimono now! – Disclose
The little budget of your woes.
You shall have both my hands to hold:
It's very late: it's very cold.

It's very cold: it's very late. The snow
Lies upon all the housetops. But we two
Have each of us such ancient work to do:
You sell caresses: I, a song or so:
And so we please each other . . . Yes, I know.
It's very late: it's very cold. The snow
Blocks all the tram-lines. Here's a pleasant ease;
Your arm-chair and a fire: curtains and peace.
And, since you rest me, lying on my knees –
When to my niche I'm hoisted – on that day
Stand up and claim your leaf of poet's bay.
Do it: be bold!
I shall not shun you in my memories;
You shall have, then as now, a hand to hold.

It's very late: it's very cold:
You keep your bargains, I'll be bold
To say, more loyally than half the men
I'll meet to-morrow, any other when
Or any other where. – My dear, that's Fate!
Run off to bed. Good-night! It's very late.

THE STARLING

It's an odd thing how one changes! . . .
Walking along the upper ranges
Of this land of plains
In this month of rains,
On a drying road where the poplars march along,
Suddenly,
With a rush of wings flew down a company,
A multitude, throng upon throng,
Of starlings,
Successive orchestras of wind-blown song,
Whirled, like a babble of surf,
On to the roadside turf –

And so, for a mile, for a mile and a half . . . a long way
Flight followed flight,
Thro' the still, grey light
Of the steel-grey day,
Whirling beside the road in clamorous crowds,
Never near, never far, in the shade of the poplars and clouds!

It's an odd thing how one changes! . . .
And what strikes me now as most strange is,
After the starlings had flown
Over the plain and were gone,
There was one of them stayed on alone
On a twig; it chattered on high,
Lifting its bill to the sky,
Distending its throat,
Crooning harsh note after note,
In soliloquy,
Sitting alone.

And, after a hush,
It gurgled as gurgles a well,
Warbled as warbles a thrush,
Had a try at the sound of a bell
And mimicked a jay . . .
But I,
Whilst the starling mimicked on high,
Pulsing its throat and its wings,

I went on my way
Thinking of things
Onwards, and over the range
And that's what is strange.

I went down 'twixt tobacco and grain,
Descending the chequerboard plain
Where the apples and maize are,
Under the loop-holed gate
In the village wall
Where the goats clatter over the cobbles
And the intricate, straw-littered ways are . . .
The ancient watchman hobbles,
Cloaked, with his glasses of horn at the end of his nose,
With velvet short hose
And a three-cornered hat on his pate,
And his pike-staff and all;
And he carries a proclamation –
An invitation
To great and small,
Man and beast,
To a wedding feast;
And he carries a bell and rings . . .
From the steeple looks down a saint,
From a doorway a queenly peasant
Looks out, in her bride gown of lace,
And her sister, a quaint little darling
Who twitters and chirps like a starling.
And this little old place,
It's so quaint,
It's so pleasant,
And the watch bell rings and the church bell rings
And the wedding procession draws nigh,
Bullock carts, fiddlers and goods;
But I
Pass on my way to the woods
Thinking of things.

Years ago, I'd have stayed by the starling,
Marking the iridescence of his throat,
Marvelling at the change in his note;
I'd have said to the peasant child; 'Darling,

Here's a groschen and give me a kiss!' . . . I'd have stayed
To sit with the bridesmaids at table
And have taken my chance
Of a dance
With the bride in her laces
Or the maids with the blond, placid faces
And ribbons and crants in the stables. . . .

But the church bell still rings
And I'm far away out on the plain,
In the grey weather among the tobacco and grain,
And the village and gate and the wall
Are a long grey line with the church over all.
And miles and miles away in the sky
The starlings go wheeling round on high
Over the distant ranges.
The violin strings
Thrill away and the day grows more grey.
And I. . . . I stand thinking of things.
Yes, it's strange how one changes! . . .

AUTUMN EVENING

The cold light dies, the candles glow,
The wind whirls down the bare allée
Outside my gleaming window-panes
The phantom populations go,
Blown, amid leaves, above, below.

Yet these are solid German folk
Outside, beneath the thinning planes
And the reflections that awoke
At candle time upon my panes
Are misty, unsubstantial gleams.

Only outside, obscurity,
The waning light, the cold blue beams
And rafts of shadow trick the eye;
So that the frozen passers-by

Look ghosts – and only real seems
My candle lighted, lonely place,
The gleaming windows and your face
Looking in likeness from the wall
Where the fantastic shadows fall. . . .

Now the ghosts pass, the cold wind cries,
The leaves sift downwards, the world dies,
But in the shadows, lo! your eyes.

IN THE TRAIN

Out of the window I see a dozen great stars, burning bright,
Flying in silence, engrossed in the uttermost depths of the night,
Star beyond star, growing clear, flying on as I pass through the night.
It's many days since last I saw the stars
Look through the night sky's bars
Like mists and veils of shimmer and shining gauze –
So little time we have and so much cause
To stay beneath the roof; so much to do!
The life we lead! . . . Well, you
Get to your bed at ten, and you, away
I like my glass of wine to end the day.

Now as the train ambles on, slowly and I watch alone
Stars and black woods and the stream, dim in the light of the stars
Winding away to the past beneath Castor and Pollux and Mars;
It seems as long since last I held your hand
As since I saw the stars.
And ah! if we meet in this land,
And ah! if we meet oversea –
In the dark where the traffic of London races
Or in these castled, woodland places –
And then – wherever it be
Shall not our thoughts go away into deeps
Where the mind sleeps and the brain too sleeps,
As when we take thought and we gaze
Past all the bee swarms of stars
Spread o'er the night and its bars,

Past mists and veils and shimmer and shine and haze
Into the deep and silent places,
The still, unfathomable spaces
Where the brain sleeps and the mind too sleeps
And all the deeps stretch out beyond the deeps
And thought dies down before infinity . . .
So, in an utter satisfaction
Beyond all thought and beyond all action
In a blindness more blind than the starless places
I shall stretch my face to where your face is.
And over head, over land and sea
Shall the white stars wheel in their reverie.

THE EXILE

My father had many oxen
    Yet all are gone;
My father had many servants;
    I sit alone.

He followed the Southern women,
    He drank of the Southern wines;
He fought in the Southern quarrels –
    My lot declines.

I will go to the Southern houses; I will sit 'mid the maids at hire;
I will bear the meat to their tables and carry wood to their fire;
Where the chink of the rat and the mouse is, all night long will I lie
Awake in the byres and the stables. . . . When the white moon looks from the sky
And over the shadowed roof-trees, and the wind blows warm from the South,
With the heavy tears on my eyelids and the weary sighs in my mouth
I shall hear through the gaping gables how the Southern night bird sings
Of the slaves who were once Queen's daughters and hinds the seed of Kings.

My father had many oxen
    Yet all are gone;
My father had many servants;
    I sit alone.

RHYMING

The bells go chiming
O'er Germany
I sit here rhyming . . .

If fun were funny,
And love lived long,
And always honey
Were sweet on the tongue,
Would life be better
Or freedom free?

If each love-letter
Spelt loyalty,
If we didn't go timing
The dance with a fetter?

If gold were true gold
For alchemists
– I sit here rhyming –
And all were new gold
In morning mists?
Would laughter measure
The step of life
If each took pleasure
In each's wife?
If much were undone
In what we see
And we built up London
In High Germany;
Without much pity
For crushed out grain
We'd fling the city
Across this plain –
A phantom city
Like old Cokayne –
Where old dead passions
Come true again
And old time fashions
Be new again,
Where jests once witty

Would start again,
And long lost pity
Take heart again.

So I sit rhyming
Of fun to be,
And the bells all go chiming
O'er High Germany.

CANZONE À LA SONATA
(To E.P.)

What do you find to boast of in our age,
To boast of now, my friendly sonneteer,
And not to blush for, later? By what line
Do you entrain from Mainz to regions saner?
Count our achievements and uplift my heart;
Blazon our fineness, Optimist, I toil
Whilst you crow cocklike. But I cannot see

What's left behind us for a heritage
For our young children? What but nameless fear?
What creeds have we to teach, legends to twine
Saner than spun our dams? Or what's there saner
That we've devised to comfort those who part,
One for some years to walk the stone-clad soil,
One to his fathom-deep bed? What coin have we

For ransom when He grimly lays his siege
Whose dart is sharpened for our final hurt?
I think we do not think; we deem more fair
Earth with unthought on death; we deem him gainer
Whose brow unshadowd shows no wrinkled trail
Of the remembrance of the countless slain;
Who sets the world to fitful melody –

To fitful minstrelsy that's summer's liege
When all the summer's sun-kissed fountains spurt
Kisses of bubbling sound about our hair.
I think we think that singing soul the gainer
Who disremembers that spent youth must fail,
That after autumn comes, few leaves remain
And all the well-heads freeze, and melody

O'er frozen waters grows too hoarse with age
To keep us from extremity of fear.
When agèd poets pen another line
And agèd maidens coif their locks in saner
And staider snoods; when winter of the heart
Comes on and beds beneath the frozen soil
Gape open – where's your grinning melody?

THE FEATHER

I wonder dost thou sleep at night,
False friend and falser enemy!
I wonder if thy hours are long and drag out wearily!
We've passed days and nights together
In our time . . . . But that white feather
That the wind's blown past the roof ridge
It is gone . . . . So I, from thee!

Aye, chase it o'er the courtyard stones.
Past friend of mine, my enemy!
Chase on beneath the chestnut boughs and out toward the sea,
If the fitful wind should fail it,
Thou may'st catch it, and may'st trail it
In midden's mud and garbage . . . .
As thou hast my thoughts of thee.

So I wonder dost thou sleep at night?
Once friend of mine, my enemy?
Or whether dost thou toss and turn to plan new treachery?
As the feather thou hast trodden
So my thoughts of thee are sodden

When I think. . . . . Yes, half forgotten,
A faint taste of something rotten
Comes at times, like worm-struck wood ash
Comes at times, the thought of thee.

But I would not have thy night thoughts
As the slow clock beats to dayward!
I'll be sleeping with my eyes shut,
Dreaming deep, or dreaming wayward.
And I hear thee turn and mutter
As thy dawn-ward candles gutter –
For thou fear'st the dark . . . Hark! 'Judas!'
Says the dawn wind from the sea.
Round the house it whispers 'Judas!'
Friend of mine, my enemy.

SÜSSMUND'S ADDRESS TO AN UNKNOWN GOD[1]
(Adapted from the High German)

My God, they say I have no bitterness!
Dear Unknown God, I gasp, I fade, I pine!
No bitterness! Have firs no turpentine?
If so, it's true.

Because I do not go wandering round Piccadilly
Like an emasculated lily
In a low-necked flannel shirt beneath the rain.
(Is that what you'd do,
Oh God Unknown,
If you came down
To Piccadilly
And worried over London town?)
Wailing round Covent Garden's what I should do
Declaiming to the beefy market porters
Dramatic propaganda about social wrongs

---

[1]   Carl Eugen Freiherr von Süssmund, b.1872 d.1910. This is of course
a quite free adaptation. [Ford's note]

Denouncing Edward Morters
Or saying that Mr William Parnett
Is eleven kinds of literary hornet,
Or that the death of Mr Arthur Mosse
Would be no sort of loss
But a distinct gain
– That sort of silly literary songs
About no one that *you* know,
And no one else could ever want to know.

You owe
(You've heard a hundred thousand *dat qui cito's*)
Some sort of poisonous dew
Shed on the flowers where these high-horned mosquitoes
Dance in a busy crew.
But they will go on setting up their schools,
Making their little rules,
Finding selected ana,
Collected in Montana:
Connected with Commedié Diviné
Or maidens with names like Devidriné . . .
Dear Lord, you know the stuff
You must have heard enough.

Find me a barrel into which to creep
Dear Unknown God, and get dead drunk and sleep.
But listen, this is for your ear alone
(God: where are you? Let me come close and whisper
What no one knows – I'm really deadly tired,
I cannot write a line, my hands are stiff,
Writing's a rotten job, my head goes round:
You have afflicted me with whip-cord nerves.
That hammering fool drives me distracted . . . God!
Strike him with colic, send him screaming home.
Strike, Dash and Dash and Dash with eye complaints;
That beast who choked his dog with a tight collar
(He gave his child the lead to hold) last night;
It made me sick; God strike him with the pip.
And send down one dark night and no one near
And one white throat within my fingers' grip!)

Dear God, you bade me be a gentleman,
And well you know I've been it. But their rot . . .
Sometimes it makes me angry. This last season
I've listened smiling to new Celtic bards,
To Anti-Vivisectionists and Friends of Peace,
To Neo-Psychics, Platonists and Poets
Who saved the Universe by chopping logs
In your own image. . . .
I've smiled at Whigs intoning Whiggery
To keep the Labour Market down; at Tories
Sickening for office. I have surely been
Plumb centre in the Movement. O my God
Is this a man's work: God I've backed up —'s
With proper letters in the Daily Press:
I've smiled at Dowagers and Nonconformists;
At wriggling dancers; forty pianists;
Jew politicians; Front Rank Statesmen's —'s
Yankee conductors of chaste magazines . . .
God, fill my purse and let me go away.

But God, dear God! I'll never get away
I know the . . . . you are!
That's off my chest. You'll never let me go.
I know I'll never drink myself dead drunk
Because to-morrow I shall have appointments
– You'll make them for me – with a Jail Reform
And Pure Milk Rotter – such a pleasant man!
One garden city builder, seven peers
Concerned with army remounts, and a girl
Mad to take dancing lessons! Such my morrow!
It's not much I ask Great God of mine
(Fill up my little purse and let me go!)
These earnest, cold-in-the-heart and practised preachers
Have worked their will on me for long enough,
Some boring me to tears while I sit patient
Some picked my purse and bit me in the back
The while I smiled as you have taught me to,
(Fill up my little purse and let me go!)

(*Note.* – I have been unable to follow the Freiherr at any interval at all
on this page without leaving several words blank. F.M.H.)

It's not my job to go denouncing jobs
You did not build me for it. Not my job!
Whilst they are on the make, snatching their bits
Beneath the wheels of ninety-nine reforms.
But this is truth:
There's not one trick they've not brought off on me,
I guess they think I haven't noticed it
For I've no bitterness . . .
They've lied about me to my mistresses,
Stolen my brandy, plagiarised my books,
Lived on me month by month, broken agreements,
Perjured themselves in courts, and sworn false oaths
With all the skill of Protestant British tradesmen
Plundering a Papist and a foreigner
With God on their lips. . . .
But all that's private. . .

                              Oh, you sleeping God,
I hope you sit amongst the coloured tents
Of any other rotten age than this –
With great pavilions tinctured all with silks,
Where emerald lawns go stretching into space,
With mailèd horses, simple drunken knights,
Punctilious heralds and high-breasted ladies
Beauteous beyond belief and not one better
Than you would have her be – in such a heaven
Where there's no feeling of the moral pulse,
I think I'd find some peace – with treachery
Of the sword and dagger kind to keep it sweet –
– Adultery, foul murder, pleasant things,
A touch of incest, theft, but no Reformers.

Dear God of mine
Who've tortured me in many pleasant ways
I hope you've had some fun. And thank you, God!
No doubt you'll keep your bargain in the end,
No doubt I'll get my twopenny-halfpenny pay
At the hack door of some bright hued pavilion
From a — [whore] of Heaven. . . .

But when it comes to 'have no bitterness' . . .
(For bitter we read 'earnest') I've no stomach
For such impertinence; its subtlety

(You know it, God, but let me get it down)
Is too ingenious. It implies just this:

'Here is a man when times are out of joint
Who will not be enraged at Edward Morter,
Parnett or Mosse; who will not to the woes
Of a grey underworld lend passionate ears
Nor tear his hair to tatters in the cause
Of garden suburbs or of guinea pigs
Injected with bacilli . . . Such a man
(So say the friends that I have listened to
Whole wasted, aching desolate afternoons!)
Is morally castrated; pass him by;
Give him no management in this great world,
No share in fruity Progress or the wrongs
Of market porters, tram conductors, pimps,
Marriage-reforming divorcés, Whig statesmen
Or serious Drama.'

Did I, dear God, ever attempt to shine
As such a friend of Progress? God, did I
Ever ambitiously raise up my voice
To out shout these eminent preachers?
Suck up importance from a pauper's wrongs
I never did!
But these mosquitoes must make precious sure
I do not take a hand in their achievements
Therefore they say, I have no bitterness
Being a eunuch amongst these proper men,
Who stand foursquare against evil (that's their phrase!)

God, you've been hard on me; I'm plagued with boils,
Little mosquito-stings, warts, poverty!
Yes, very hard. But when all's catalogued
You've been a gentleman in all your fun.
No doubt you'll keep your bargain, Unknown God.
This surely you will never do to me –
Say I'm not bitter. That you'll never do.
T'would be to outpass the bounds of the Divine
And turn Reformer.

IN THE LITTLE OLD MARKET-PLACE
(To the Memory of A.V.)

It rains, it rains,
From gutters and drains
And gargoyles and gables:
It drips from the tables
That tell us the tolls upon grains,
Oxen, asses, sheep, turkeys and fowls
Set into the rain-soaked wall
Of the old Town Hall.

The mountains being so tall
And forcing the town on the river,
The market's so small
That, with the wet cobbles, dark arches and all,
The owls
(For in dark rainy weather the owls fly out
Well before four), so the owls
In the gloom
Have too little room
And brush by the saint on the fountain
In veering about.

The poor saint on the fountain!
Supported by plaques of the giver
To whom we're beholden;
His name was de Sales
And his wife's name von Mangel.
(Now is he a saint or archangel?)
He stands on a dragon
On a ball, on a column
Gazing up at the vines on the mountain:
And his falchion is golden.
And his wings are all golden.
He bears golden scales
And in spite of the coils of his dragon, without hint of alarm or invective
Looks up at the mists on the mountain.

(Now what saint or archangel
Stands winged on a dragon,
Bearing golden scales and a broad bladed sword all golden?

Alas, my knowledge
Of all the saints of the college,
Of all these glimmering, olden
Sacred and misty stories
Of angels and saints and old glories . . .
Is sadly defective.)
The poor saint on the fountain . . .

On top of his column
Gazes up sad and solemn.
But is it towards the top of the mountain
Where the spindrifty haze is
That he gazes?
Or is it into the casement
Where the poor girl sits sewing?
There's no knowing.

Hear it rain!
And from eight leaden pipes in the ball he stands on,
That has eight leaden and copper bands on,
There gurgle and drain
Eight driblets of water down into the basin.
And he stands on his dragon
And the girl sits sewing
High, very high in her casement
And before her are many geraniums in a parket
All growing and blowing
In box upon box
From the gables right ˙down to the basement
With the frescoes and carvings and paint . . .

The poor saint!
It rains and it rains,
In the market there isn't an ox,
And in all the emplacement
For waggons there isn't a waggon,
Not a stall for a grape or a raisin,
Not a soul in the market
Save the saint on his dragon
With the rain dribbling down in the basin,
And the maiden that sews in the casement.

They are still and alone,
Mutterseelens alone,
And the rain dribbles down from his heels and his crown,
From wet stone to wet stone.
It's as grey as at dawn,
And the owls, grey and fawn,
Call from the little town hall
With its arch in the wall,
Where the fire-hooks are stored.

From behind the flowers of her casement
That's all gay with the carvings and paint,
The maiden gives a great yawn,
But the poor saint –
No doubt he's as bored!
Stands still on his column
Uplifting his sword
With never the ease of a yawn
From wet dawn to wet dawn . . .

TO ALL THE DEAD

I

A Chinese Queen on a lacquered throne
With a dragon as big as the side of a house,
All golden, and silent and sitting alone
In an empty house.

With the shadows above and the shadows behind,
And the Queen with a paper white, rice white face,
As still as a partridge, as still as a mouse,
With slanting eyes you would say were blind
In a dead, white face.

And what does she think, and what does she see,
With her face as still as a frozen pool is,
And her air as old as the oldest sea,
Where the oldest ice of the frozen Pole is?

She should have been dead nine thousand years . . .
But there come in three score and sixty coolies
With a veil of lawn as large as a lake,
And the veil blows here and shimmers there
In the unseen winds of the shadowy house.
And dragons flew in the shadowy air,
And there were chrysanthemums everywhere,
And butterflies and a coral snake
All round the margin of the lake.

For the Prince has come to court the Queen
Still sitting on high on her lacquered throne
With the golden dragon: and all the sheen
And shimmer and shine of a thousand wantons
In silken stuffs, with ivory lutes
And slanting eyes and furred blue boots
That moved in the light of a thousand lanthorns . . .

It all dies down, and the Queen sits there,
She should have been dead nine thousand years.

II

Now it happened that in the course of to-day
(The Queen was last night) in the rue de la Paix
In a room that was old and darkish and musty,
For most of the rooms are quaintly cranky
In the rue de la Paix,
For when it was new the Grande Armée
Tramped all its legions down this way.

But I sat there, and a friendly Yankee
Was lecturing me on the nature of things
(It's a way Americans have!) He was cranky,
Just as much as his rooms and his chairs and his tables.
But the window stood open and over the way
I saw the the house with the modernest facings
Had an old tiled roof with mansards and gables.
It housed a jeweller, two modistes,
A vendor of fans; and the topmost sign
Announced in a golden double line
A salon of Chinese chiropodists.

And that's Paris from heel to crown
Plate-glass in the street and jewels and lacings
And cranky rooms on the upper floors
With rusty locks and creaking doors

But of what my American friend was saying
I haven't a thought – there was too much noise
Through the open windows – the motors braying,
The clatter of hoofs in a steady stream,
And a scream
Unceasing from twenty paper boys,
With twenty versions to take your choice,
In styles courageous or gay or rococco,
Of clamorous news about Morocco . . .

III
And suddenly he said: 'Sandusky!'
Now what was he talking of there in his musky,
Worm-eaten rooms of the rue de la Paix?
– Of his youth of jack rabbits and peanuts and snakes
When all was silent about the Lakes.
Now what is the name of them? Lake Ladoga?
No, no, that's in Russia. It's Ticonderoga,
Ontario, Champlin, each with their woods,
And never a house for miles and miles
And the boys in their boats floated on by the piles
Of old wigwams where shreds of blankets dangled.
And they caught their jack rabbits, lit bonfires and angled
In shallows for catfish. That's it, in Sandusky!
The Bay of Sandusky.

And then I remembered with grey, clear precision,
And I saw – yes I saw – looking over the way
Two Chinese chiropodists, villainous fellows,
With faces of sulphur and lemon yellow,
Gaze with that gaze that's half fanatic,
Part atrocious and partly sweet,
Each from a window of his own attic
At a mannequin on my side of the street,
And each grinned and girned in his Manchester blue,
And smirked with his eyes and his pig-tail too.

And somehow they made me feel sick; but I lost them
At the word 'Sandusky.' A landscape crossed them;
A scene no more nor less than a vision,
All clear and grey in the rue de la Paix.

It must have been seven years ago,
I was out on a river whose name I've forgotten;
The Hudson perhaps or the Kotohotten.
It doesn't much matter. Do you know the Hudson?
A sort of Moselle with New York duds on,
There are crags and castles, a distance all grey,
Rocks, forests and elbows. But castles of Jay
And William H. Post and Mrs Poughkeepsie –
Imagine a Moselle that's thoroughly tipsy,
A nightmare of ninety American castles
With English servants trained up like vassals,
Of Hiram P. Ouese who's a fortune from pills for the liver.

Anyhow, I've forgotten the name of the river.

And the steamer steamed upwards between the hills
And passed through the rapids they called the Narrows
'Twixt the high grey banks where the firs grow jagged,
And the castles ceased and the forest grew ragged,
And the steamer belched forth sparks and stayed
At a wooden village, then grunted and swayed
Out to midstream and round a reach
Where the river widened and swirled about,
And we slowed in the current where black snags stuck out,
And suddenly we saw a beach –
A grey old beach and some old grey mounds
That seemed to silence the steamer's sounds;
So still and old and grey and ragged.
For there they lay, the tumuli, barrows,
The Indian graves. . . .

IV

And it wasn't so much the wampumed Braves,
Eagle feathers, jade axes and totems and arrows
That I thought about, for ten minutes later
I was up and away from the Rue de la Paix

In a train for Trêves.
But the word 'Sandusky' still hung in my brain
As we went through the greeny grey Lorraine
In a jolting train,
And then bargained for rooms with a German waiter.
Or it wasn't even in great concern
For the fate of 'Sandusky Bay.' – My friend
Pictured it thronged with American villas,
Dutch Porticos and Ionic pillars.
So that no boy's boat can land on the shores,
For the high-bred owners of dry goods stores
Forbid the practice. The villa lawns,
Pitch-pine canoes with America's daughters
In a sort of a daily Henley regatta
Are the bright parasols of Japanese paper
Keep up a ceaseless, endless chatter,
In the endless, ceaseless girl graduate story
Where once there were silence, jack-rabbits and snakes,
And o'er all the gay clatter there floats old Glory –
The flag of the States, from a calico shop.

But stop!
I am not lamenting about the Lakes.

For, as grey dawns roll on to grey dawns,
Some things must surely come to an end,
Even old silences over old waters
Even here in Trêves the Porta Nigra
That isn't so much a gaunt black ruin,
As a great black whole – a Roman gate-way,
As high as a mountain, as black as a jail –
Even here, even here, America's daughters,
Long toothed old maids with a camera
(For even they must know decay,
And the passage of time, hasting, hasting away!)
And the charm of the past grows meagre and meagre.
Though through it all the Porta Nigra
Keeps its black, hard and grim completeness,
As if no fleet minutes with all their fleetness
Could rub down its surface.
But we've walled it in in a manner of speaking
With electric trams that go sparking and streaking

And filling the night with squeals and jangles
As iron wheels grind on iron angles. . . .

And nobody cares and nobody grieves
And all the spires and towers of Trêves
Shade upwards into the sooty skies,
And you dig up here a sword or a chalice,
Some bones, some teeth and some golden bangles
And several bricks from the Caesar's Palace.

V

And so I come back to this funny old town
Where professors argue each other down,
And every one is in seven movements
For every kind of Modern Improvements;
And there isn't a moment of real ease,
But students come from the seven seas
And we boast a professor of Neo-Chinese –
A thing to astonish the upland heather –
And more than the universities
Of all High Germany put together
Can show the like of.
The upland heather
It stretches for miles and miles and miles
Wine-purple and brooding and ancient and blasted,
An endless trackless, heather forest
And so, between whiles,
When my mind's all reeling with Modern Movements
And my eyes are weary, my head at its sorest
And the best of beer has lost its zest,
I go up there to get a rest
And think of the dead. . . .

For it's nothing but dead and dead and dying
Dead faiths, dead loves, lost friends and the flying,
Fleet minutes that change and ruin our shows,
And the dead leaves flitter and autumn goes,
And the dead leaves flitter down thick to the ground,
And pomps go down and queens go down
And time flows on, and flows and flows.

But don't mistake me, the leaves are wet
And most of their copper splendour is rotten
Like most of the dead – and still and forgotten,
And I don't feel a spark of regret
Not a spark. . . .

I am sitting up here on a sort of a mound
And the dull red sun has just done sinking
And it's grown by this woodside fully dark
And I'm just thinking. . . .
And the valley lands and the forests and tillage
Are wrapped in mist. There's the lights of a village,
Of one – of three – of four! –
Four I can count from this high old mound . . .
In Tilly's time you could count eighteen . . .
You know of Tilly? A general
Who ravaged this land. There was Prince Eugene,
And Marshal Saxe and Wallenstein,
And God knows who . . . They are dead men all
With tombs in cathedrals here and there,
Just food for tourists. It's rather funny,
They ravaged these cornfields and burned the hamlets,
They drove off the cattle and took the honey,
And clocks and coin and chests and camlets:
Reduced the numbers to four from eighteen;
You can see four glimmers of light thro' the gloom.
But as for Marshal Wallenstein,
No doubt he's somewhere in some old tomb
With marble pillow beneath his head.
He was shot. Or he wasn't. Anyhow he's dead!
And I'm sitting here on an old, smashed mound.
And the wood-leaves are flittering down to the ground.
And I'm sitting here and just thinking and wondering,
Clear thoughts and pictures, dull thoughts and blundering.
It's all one. But I wonder . . . I wonder . . .

And under
The earth of the barrow there's something moving
Or no – not moving. Yes, shoving, shoving,
Through the thick, dark earth – a fox or a mole.
Phui! But it's dark! I can't grasp the whole
Of my argument – No. I'm not dropping to sleep!

(I can hear the leaves in the dark, cold wood!
That's a boar by his rustling!) *'From good to good,*
And good to better you say we go.'
(There's an owl overhead.) *'You say that's so?'*
My American friend of the rue de la Paix?
'Grow better and better from day to day.'
Well, well I had a friend that's not a friend to-day;
Well, well, I had a love who's resting in the clay
Of a suburban cemetery. *'Friend,*
My Yankee friend.' (He's mighty heavy and tusky,
Judged by his rustlings, that old boar in the wood)
'From good to good.
Have you found a better bay than old Sandusky?
Or I a better friend than the one that's left me?'
'No Argument? – Well I'm not arguing
I came out here to think' –
Now what's that thing
That's coursing o'er dead leaves. It's not a boar!
Some sort of woman! A Geheimrath's cook
Come out to meet her lover of the Ninth –.
An Uhlan Regiment! You know the Uhlans,
Who charged at Mars La Tour; that's on their colours.

But that little wretch.
Whoever heard such kissing! Sighs now! Groans!
In the copper darkness of these wet, high forests.
Well, well, that's no affair of mine to-night.
I came out here though, yes, I'd an engagement
With Major Hahn to give him his revenge –
What was it? At roulette? But I'd a headache!
I came out here to think about that Queen!
The Chinese one – the one I saw in Paris.
To-night's the thirtieth. . . the thirty-first.
Why, yes, it's All Soul's Eve. That's why I'm morbid
With thoughts of All the Dead. . . That Chinese Queen
She never kissed her lover. But a queer,
A queer, queer look came out on her rice white face!
I never knew such longing was in the world,
Though not a feature stirred in her! No kisses!
But there she wavered just behind his back
With her slanting eyes. No moth about a flame,
No seabird in the storm round a lighthouse glare

Was e'er so lured to the ruin and wreck of love.
And he knelt there with such a queer, queer face
A queer, queer smile, and his uplifted hands
– He prayed as we pray to a Queen in dragon silk
– His hands rubbed palm on palm. And so she swayed
And swayed just like a purple butterfly
Above the open jaws of a coral snake.

But she
Should have been dead nine thousand years and more,
Says our Chinese professor. For such acting
Was proper to the days and time of TSüang:
It's hopelessly demoded, dead and gone!
To-day we have – Chinese chiropodists
Who smile like toads at Paris mannequins
In the sacred name of Progress. Well, well, well!
I'm not regretting it – No vain regrets!
What's that. . . .

Out of the loom of the Philosopher's wood
Two figures brushing on the frozen grass.
The Uhlan and the cook. So I cried out:
'So late at night and not yet in the barracks!
Aren't you afraid of ghosts? . . . 'Oh ghosts! oh ghosts,'
I got my answer: 'Friend,
In our old home the air's so thick with ghosts
You couldn't breathe if they were an objection!'
And so I said: 'Well, well!' to make them pass. . . .

Just a glimmer of light there was across the grass
And on my barrow mound. Upon his head
The gleam of a helmet, and some sort of pelt
About his shoulders and the loom of a spear.
You never know these German regiments,
The oddest uniforms they have; and as for her
Her hair was all across her shoulders and her face,
Woodland embraces bring the hairpins out . . .
'My friend,' I said, 'you'd better hurry home
Or else you'll lose your situation!' They
Bickered in laughter and the man just said:
'You're sitting on it!'
So I moved a little,

Apologetically, just as if
It was his table in a restaurant.
So he said calmly, looking down at me:
'They call these mounds the Hunnen Gräber – Graves
Of Huns – a modern, trifling folk!
We've slept in them well on nine thousand years
My wife and I. The dynasty TSüang
Then reigned in China – well, you know their ways
Of courting. But your specialty just now
I understand's not human life but death.
I died with a wolf at my throat, this woman here
With a sword in her stomach. Yes she fell on it
To keep me company in that tumulus.
Millions and millions of dead there lie round here
In the manoeuvre grounds of the Seventeenth.
Oh, yes, I'm up to date, why not, why not?
When they've the Sappers here in garrison
The silly chaps come digging in these mounds
For practice; but they've not got down to us.
The Seventeenth just scutter up and down
At scaling practice and that's rather fun.
There was a sergeant took a chap by the ear
Last year and threw him bodily down the mound;
Then the recruit up with his bayonet
And stuck him through the neck – no end of things
We find for gossip in nine thousand years!
A Mongol people? Yes of course we were
I knew her very well that Queen who loved,
With the rice white face – 'Ta-why' 's her proper name
And that adultery bred heaps of trouble!
You've heard of Troy? Tra-hai's the real name
As Ta-why's Helen. Well, you know all that?
That trouble sent us here, being burnt out
By the King called Ko-ha! And we wandered on
In just ten years of burning towns. This slave
My wife came from Irkutsk way to the east
Where the tundra is – You know the nightingales
Come there in spring, and so they buried us
Finger to finger as the ritual is.
Not know the ritual? Well, a mighty chief
Is buried in a chamber like a room
Walled round with slabs of stone. But mighty lovers

Lie on their backs at both arms' length, so far
That just each little finger touches. Well
That's how they buried us. A hundred years
It took to get accustomed to the change.
We lay just looking up – just as you might
Upwards through quiet water at the stars,
The roots of the grass, and other buryings,
Lying remembering and touching fingers.
Just still and quiet. Then I heard a whisper
Lasting a hundred years or so; 'Your lips,'
It said, 'Your lips! your lips! your lips!' And then
It might have been five more score years. I felt
Her fingers crawling, crawling, up my wrist.
And always the voice, call, calling; 'Give your lips!'

It must have taken me a thousand years
– The Dead are patient – just to know that she
Was calling for my lips. What an embrace!
My God what an embrace was ours through the Earth!
My friend, if you should chance to meet Old Death
That unprogressive tyrant, tell him this,
He execrates my name – but tell him this –
He calls me Radical! Red Socialist,
That sort of thing. But you just tell him this,
The revolutionary leader of his realms
Got his ambition from his dead girl's lips.
Tell him in future he should spare hot lovers,
Though that's too late! We're working through the earth,
By the score, by the million. Half his empire's lost.
How can he fight us? He has but one dart
For every lover of the sons of Ahva!
You call her Eve. This is a vulgar age. . .'

And so beside the woodland in the sheen
And shimmer of the dewlight, crescent moon
And dew wet leaves I heard the cry 'Your lips!
Your lips! Your lips!' It shook me where I sat
It shook me like a trembling, fearful reed,
The call of the dead. A multitudinous
And shadowy host glimmered and gleamed,
Face to face, eye to eye, heads thrown back, and lips
Drinking, drinking from lips, drinking from bosoms

The coldness of the dew – and all a gleam
Translucent, moonstruck as of moving glasses,
Gleams on dead hair, gleams on the white dead shoulders
Upon the backgrounds of black purple woods. . .

There came great rustlings from the copper leaves
And pushing outwards, shouldering, a boar
With seven wives – a monstrous tusky brute.
I rose and rubbed my eyes and all eight fled
Tore down the mountain through the thick of the leaves
Like a mighty wave of the sea that poured itself
Farther and farther down the listening night.
All round me was the clearing, and white mist
Shrouded the frosty tussocks of old grass.
And in the moonlight a wan fingerpost
(I could not read the lower row of words.)
Proclaimed: 'Forbidden!' That's High Germany.
Take up your glasses. 'Prosit!' to the past
To all the Dead!

GOTHICISMS†

I. *The White Raven*
You are a white crow; you are a surgical scalpel;
You have taken my manhood – I shall never see sunlight again
Since you have had out my eyes.
You! You!
May Fate be very kind to you; kindest among women!

II. *The Mouldering Corpse*
I am a mouldering corpse
Deep down;
You, two whispering hyaenas.
Every night comes the brush of your claws in the sand
Above me.
Ahi! Ahi!
Eee. . . You have hold of my armbones.
May the marrow be very tasty to you two,
Tasty and green and putrescent!

I

GLOOM!
An October like November;
August a hundred thousand hours,
And all September,
A hundred thousand, dragging sunlit days,
And half October like a thousand years . . .
And doom!
That then was Antwerp. . .
                    In the name of God,
How could they do it?
Those souls that usually dived
Into the dirty caverns of mines;
Who usually hived
In whitened hovels; under ragged poplars;
Who dragged muddy shovels, over the grassy mud,
Lumbering to work over the greasy sods. . .
Those men there, with the appearances of clods
Were the bravest men that a usually listless priest of God
Ever shrived. . .
And it is not for us to make them an anthem.
If we found words there would come no wind that would fan them
To a tune that the trumpets might blow it,
Shrill through the heaven that's ours or yet Allah's
Or the wide halls of any Valhallas.
We can make no such anthem. So that all that is ours
For inditing in sonnets, pantoums, elegiacs, or lays
Is this:
'In the name of God how could they do it?'

II

For there is no new thing under the sun,
Only this uncomely man with a smoking gun
In the gloom. . .
What the devil will he gain by it?
Digging a hole in the mud and standing all day in the rain by it
Waiting his doom,
The sharp blow, the swift outpouring of the blood,
Till the trench of grey mud

Is turned to a brown purple drain by it.
Well, there have been scars
Won in many wars . . .
Punic,
Lacedæmonian, wars of Napoleon, wars for faith, wars
    for honour, for love, for possession,
But this Belgian man in his ugly tunic,
His ugly round cap, shooting on, in a sort of obsession,
Overspreading his miserable land,
Standing with his wet gun in his hand . . .
Doom!
He finds that in a sudden scrimmage
And lies, an unsightly lump on the sodden grass . . .
An image that shall take long to pass!

III

For the white-limbed heroes of Hellas ride by upon their horses
Forever through our brains.
The heroes of Cressy ride by upon their stallions;
And battalions and battalions and battalions –
The Old Guard, the Young Guard, the men of Minden and of Waterloo,
Pass, for ever staunch,
Stand for ever true;
And the small man with the large paunch,
And the grey coat, and the large hat, and the hands behind the back,
Watches them pass
In our minds for ever . . .
But that clutter of sodden corses
On the sodden Belgian grass –
That is a strange new beauty.

IV

With no especial legends of marchings or triumphs or duty,
Assuredly that is the way of it,
The way of beauty . . .
And that is the highest word you can find to say of it.
For you cannot praise it with words
Compounded of lyres and swords,
But the thought of the gloom and the rain
And the ugly coated figure, standing beside a drain,

Shall eat itself into your brain:
And you will say of all heroes: 'They fought like the Belgians!'
And you will say: 'He wrought like a Belgian his fate out of gloom,'
And you will say: 'He bought like a Belgian his doom.'
And that shall be an honourable name;
'Belgian' shall be an honourable word,
As honourable as the fame of the sword,
As honourable as the mention of the many-chorded lyre,
And his old coat shall seem as beautiful as the fabrics woven in Tyre.

V

And what in the world did they bear it for?
I don't know.
And what in the world did they dare it for?
Perhaps that is not for the likes of me to understand.
They could very well have watched a hundred legions go
Over their fields and between their cities
Down into more southerly regions.
They could very well have let the legions pass through their woods,
And have kept their lives and their wives and their children
        and cattle and goods.
I don't understand.
Was it just love of their land?
Oh poor dears!
Can any man so love his land?
Give them a thousand thousand pities
And rivers and rivers of tears
To wash off the blood from the cities of Flanders.

VI

This is Charing Cross;
It is midnight;
There is a great crowd
And no light.
A great crowd, all black that hardly whispers aloud.
Surely, that is a dead woman – a dead mother!
She has a dead face;
She is dressed all in black;
She wanders to the bookstall and back,
At the back of the crowd;

And back again and again back,
She sways and wanders.

This is Charing Cross;
It is one o'clock.
There is still a great cloud, and very little light;
Immense shafts of shadows over the black crowd
That hardly whispers aloud. . .
And now! . . That is another dead mother,
And there is another and another and another . .
And little children, all in black,
All with dead faces, waiting in all the waiting-places,
Wandering from the doors of the waiting-room
In the dim gloom.
These are the women of Flanders.
They await the lost.
They await the lost that shall never leave the dock;
They await the lost that shall never again come by the train
To the embraces of all these women with dead faces;
They await the lost who lie dead in trench and barrier and foss,
In the dark of the night.
This is Charing Cross; it is past one of the clock;
There is very little light.

There is so much pain.

L'Envoi
And it was for this that they endured this gloom;
This October like November,
That August like a hundred thousand hours,
And that September,
A hundred thousand dragging sunlit days,
And half October like a thousand years. . .
Oh poor dears!

ETERNITY
Tempo Guisto
['WHEN THE WORLD WAS IN BUILDING . . . .']

Thank goodness, the moving is over;
They've swept up the straw in the passage
And life will begin. . .
. . This little, silly, tiled, white, tiny
Cottage by the bridge. . .
When we've had tea I will punt you
To Paradise for the sugar and onions.
We'll drift home in the twilight;
The trout will be rising. . .

['WHEN THE WORLD CRUMBLED']

Above a purple sea,
Wide, wide!
Once there were ivy crowns
And myrtle and cyclamen
And a god watched. . . .
And thou, oh Lesbian. . .

Well, that's all done!

THE SILVER MUSIC

In Chepstow stands a castle –
My love and I went there.
The foxgloves on the wall all heard
Her footsteps on the stair.

The sun was high in heaven,
And the perfume in the air
Came from purple cat's-valerian . . .
But her footsteps on the stair
Made a sound like silver music
Through the perfume in the air.

Oh I'm weary for the castle,
And I'm weary for the Wye;
And the flowered walls are purple,
And the purple walls are high,
And above the cat's-valerian
The foxgloves brush the sky.
But I must plod along the road
That leads to Germany.

And another soldier fellow
Shall come courting of my dear;
And it's I shall not be with her
With my lips beside her ear.
For it's he shall walk beside her
In the perfume of the air
To the silver, silver music
Of her footstep on the stair.

[Cardiff Castle, 3/7/16]

NOSTALGIA [THE IRON MUSIC]

The French guns roll continuously
And our guns, heavy, slow.
Along the Ancre, sinuously,
The transport wagons go,
And the dust is on the thistles
And the larks sing up on high . . .
But I see the Golden Valley
Down by Chepstow on the Wye.

For it's just nine weeks last Sunday
That we took the Chepstow train,
And I'm wondering if one day
We shall take that train again;
For the four point two's come screaming
Thro' the sausages on high . . .
So there's little use in dreaming
How we walked above the Wye.

Dust and corpses in the thistles
Where the gas-shells burst like snow,
And the shrapnel screams and whistles
On the Bécourt road below,
And the High Wood bursts and bristles
And the mine-clouds foul the sky . . .
But I'm with you up at Wyndcroft,
Over Tintern on the Wye.

[Albert, 22/7/16]

A SOLIS ORTUS CARDINE

Oh quiet peoples sleeping bed by bed
Beneath grey roof-trees in the glimmering West,
We who can see the silver grey and red
Rise over No Man's Land – salute your rest.

Oh quiet comrades, sleeping in the clay
Beneath a turmoil you need no more mark,
We who have lived through yet another day
Salute your graves at setting in of dark.

And rising from your beds or from the clay
You, dead, or far from lines of slain and slayers,
Thro' your eternal or your finite day
Give us our prayers!

[Ypres Salient, 6/9/16]

THE OLD HOUSES OF FLANDERS

The old houses of Flanders,
They watch by the high cathedrals;
They have eyes, mourful, tolerant and sardonic, for the ways of men,
In the high, white, tiled gables.
The rain and the night have settled down on Flanders;

It is all wet darkness; you can see nothing.
Then those old eyes, mournful, tolerant and sardonic,
Look at great, sudden, red lights,
Look upon the shades of the cathedral
And the golden rods of the illuminated rain,
For a second . . . .
And those old eyes,
Very old eyes that have watched the ways of men for generations,
Close for ever.
The high white shoulders of the gables
Slouch together for a consultation,
Slant drunkenly over in the lea of the flaming cathedrals.
They are no more, the old houses of Flanders.

ONE LAST PRAYER

I
Let me wait, my dear:
One more day:
Let me linger near,
Let me stay.
Do not bar the gate
Or draw the blind
Or lock the door that yields,
Dear. . . . be kind.

II
I have only you beneath the skies
To rest my eyes
From the cruel green of the fields
And the cold white seas
And the weary hills
And the naked trees.
I have known the hundred ills
Of the hated wars. . . .
Do not close the blind
Or draw the bars.
I have only you beneath the stars.
Dear, be kind!

[17/12/17]

I *Pte. Barnes*
He said: 'I love her for her sense
And for her quiet innocence,
And since she bears without complaint
An anxious life of toil and care
As if she were a fireside saint. . . .

'And so her quiet eyes ensnare
My eyes all day and fill my sense
And take
My thoughts all day away from other things; and keep
Me, when I should be fast asleep,
Awake!'

II *L.-Cpl. Selfe*
. . . And when she went his patience broke
And his outrageous, restless spirit woke
To a sort of mutiny against Fate . . .
                          He'd soak and soak
For nights. And he went courting a bad girl
Who sponged on him and kept him in a whirl
And brought
Him into many questionable homes.
It's that way ruin comes.
So we all thought
He'd go to Hell – or certainly be broke . . .
But he got off with just an inch to spare –
The breadth of a hair!

III *Cpl. Bavler*
(Corporal in charge of Regimental Gardens)
He thought: 'If she would be my wife,
And live where I do set and class
My plants: when I was not on duty,
We'd live a pleasant, quiet life,
For I'd take pleasure in her beauty,
Strolling amongst the plants in order
And stopping by the potherb border.'

[18-21/12/17]

FOOTSLOGGERS
    To C.F.G.M.

I

What is love of one's land? . . .
                    I don't know very well.
It is something that sleeps
For a year – or a day –
For a month – something that keeps
Very hidden and quiet and still
And then takes
The quiet heart like a wave,
The quiet brain like a spell,
The quiet will
Like a tornado; and that shakes
The whole of the soul.

II

It is omnipotent like love;
It is deep and quiet as the grave
And it awakes
Like a flame, like a madness,
Like the great passion of your life.
The cold keenness of a tempered knife,
The great gladness of a wedding day,
The austerity of monks who wake to pray
In the dim light,
Who pray
In the darkling grove,
All these and a great belief in what we deem the right
Creeping upon us like the overwhelming sand,
Driven by a December gale,
Make up the love of one's land.

III

            But I ask you this:
About the middle of my first Last Leave,
I stood on a kerb in the pitch of the night
Waiting for buses that didn't come
To take me home.

That was in Paddington.
The soot-black night was over one like velvet:
And one was very alone – so very alone
In the velvet cloak of the night.
                              Like a lady's skirt,
A dim, diaphanous cone of white, the rays
Of a shaded street lamp, close at hand, existed,
And there was nothing but vileness it could show,
Vile, pallid faces drifted through, chalk white;
Vile alcoholic voices in the ear, vile fumes
From the filthy pavements . . . vileness!

                    And one thought:
'In three days' time we enter the unknown:
And this is what we die for!'
                    For, mind you,
It isn't just a Tube ride, going to France!
It sets ironic unaccustomed minds
At work even in the sentimental . . .
                              Still
All that is in the contract.

IV
                    Who of us
But has, deep down in the heart and deep in the brain
The memory of odd moments: memories
Of huge assemblies chanting in the night
At palace gates: of drafts going off in the rain
To shaken music: or the silken flutter
Of silent, ceremonial parades,
In the sunlight, when you stand so stiff to attention,
That you never see but only know they are there –
The regimental colours – silken, a-flutter
Azure and gold and vermilion against the sky:
The sacred finery of banded hearts
Of generations. . . .
                    And memories
When just for moments, landscapes out in France
Looked so like English downlands that the heart
Checked and stood still. . . .

Or then, the song and dance
Of Battalion concerts, in the shafts of light ·
From smoky lamps: the lines of queer, warped faces
Of men that are now dead: faces lit up
By inarticulate minds at sugary chords
From the vamping pianist beneath the bunting:
'Until the boys come home!' we sing. And fumes
Of wet humanity, soaked uniforms,
Wet flooring, smoking lamps, fill cubical
And wooden-walled spaces, brown, all brown,
With the light-sucking hue of the khaki. . . .And the rain
Frets on the pitchpine of the felted roof
Like women's fingers beating on a door
Calling 'Come Home' . . . 'Come Home'
Down the long trail beneath the silent moon . . . .
Who never shall come. . . .
        And we stand up to sing
'Hen wlad fy nadhau. . . .'
          Dearest, never one
Of your caresses, dearest in the world,
Shall interpenetrate the flesh of one's flesh,
The breath of the lungs, sight of the eyes, or the heart,
Like that sad, harsh anthem in the rained-on huts
Of our own men . . .
That too is in the contract. . . .

V

        Well, of course
One loves one's men. One takes a mort of trouble
To get them spick and span upon parades:
You straf them, slang them, mediate between
Their wives and loves, and you inspect their toe-nails
And wangle leaves for them from the Adjutant
Until your Company office is your home
And all your mind. . . .
        This is the way it goes:
First your Platoon and then your Company,
Then the Battalion then Brigade, Division,
And the whole B.E.F. in France . . . and then
Our Land, with its burden of civilians,
Who take it out of us as little dogs

Worry Newfoundlands. . . .
                    So, in the Flanders mud,
We bear the State upon our rain-soaked backs,
Breathe life into the State from our rattling lungs,
Anoint the State with the rivulets of sweat
From our tin helmets.
                    And so, in years to come
The State shall take the semblance of Britannia,
Up-borne, deep-bosomed, with anointed limbs . . .
Like the back of a penny.

VI

                    For I do not think
We ever took much stock in that Britannia
On the long French roads, or even on parades,
Or thought overmuch of Nelson or of Minden,
Or even the old traditions. . . .
                    I don't know,
In the breathless rush that is of parades and drills,
Of digging at the double and strafes and fatigues,
These figures grow dimmed and lost
Doubtless we too, we too, when the years have receded
Shall look like the heroes of Hellas upon a frieze,
White-limbed and buoyant and passing the flame of the torches
From hand to hand. . . . But to-day it's mud to the knees
And khaki and khaki and khaki. . . .
                    And the love of one's land
Very quiet and hidden and still. . . . And again
I don't know, though I've pondered the matter for years
Since the war began. . . . But I never had much brain. . . .

VII

I don't know if you know the 1.10 train
From Cardiff:
                    Well, fourteen of us together
Went up from Cardiff in the summer weather
At the time of the July push.
It's a very good train;
It runs with hardly a jar and never a stop
After Newport, until you get down

In London Town.
It goes with a solemn, smooth rush
Across the counties and over the shires,
Right over England past farmsteads and byres;
It bubbles with conversation,
Being the West going to the East:
The pick of the rich of the West in a bunch,
Half of the wealth of the Nation,
With heads together, buzzing of local topics,
Of bankrupts and strikes, divorces and marriages;
And, after Newport, you get your lunch,
In the long, light, gently swaying carriages
As the miles flash by,
And fields and flowers
Flash by
Under the high sky
Where the great cloud towers
Above the tranquil downs
And the tranquil towns.

VIII

And the corks pop
And the wines of France
Bring in radiance;
And spice from the tropics
Flavours fowl from the Steppes
And meat from the States,
And the talk buzzes on like bees round the skeps,
And the potentates
Of the mines and the docks
Drink delicate hocks . . .
Ah, proud and generous civilisation. . . .

IX

For me, going out to France
Is like the exhaustion of dawn
After a dance. . . .
You have rushed around to get your money,
To get your revolver, complete your equipment;
You have had your moments, sweeter – ah, sweeter than honey;

You have got your valise all ready for shipment:
You have gone to confession and wangled your blessing,
You have bought your air-pillow and sewn in your coat
A pocket to hold your first field-dressing,
And you've paid the leech who bled you, the vampire . . .
And you've been to the Theatre and the Empire,
And you've bidden good-bye to the band and the goat . . .
And, like a shop that floats free of her berth,
There's nothing that holds you now to the earth,
And you're near enough to a yawn. . . .
'Good luck' and 'Good-bye' it has been, and 'So long, old chap'
'Cheerio: you'll be back in a month' – 'You'll have driven
        the Huns off the map.'
And one little pressure of the hand
From the thing you love next to the love of the land,
Since you leave her, out of love of your land. . . .
But that little, long, gentle and eloquent pressure
Shall go with you under the whine of the shells,
Into the mire and the stress,
Into the seven hundred hells,
Until you come down on your stretcher
To the C.C.S. . . .
And back to Blighty again –
Or until you go under the sod.

X

But, in the 1.10 train,
Running between the green and the grain,
Something like the peace of God
Descended over the hum and the drone
Of the wheels and the wine and the buzz of the talk,
And one thought:
'In two days' time we enter the Unknown,
And this is what we die for!'
And thro' the square
Of glass
At my elbow, as limpid as air,
I watched our England pass
The great downs moving slowly,
Far away,
The farmsteads quiet and lowly,

Passing away;
The fields newly mown
With the swathes of hay,
And the wheat just beginning to brown,
Whirling away. . . .
And I thought
'In two days' time we enter the Unknown,
But *this* is what we die for. . . . As we ought. . . .'
For it is for the sake of the wolds and the wealds
That we die,
And for the sake of the quiet fields,
And the path through the stackyard gate . . .
That these may be inviolate,
And know no tread save those of the herds and the hinds,
And that the south-west winds
Blow on no forehead save of those that toil
On our suave and hallowed soil,
And that deep peace may rest
Upon that quiet breast. . . .
It is because our land is beautiful and green and comely,
Because our farms are quiet and thatched and homely,
Because the trout stream dimples by the willow,
Because the water-lilies float upon the ponds,
And on Eston Hill the delicate, waving fronds
Of the bracken put forth, where the white clouds are flying,
That we shall endure the swift, sharp torture of dying,
Or the humiliation of not dying,
Where the gas cloud wanders
Over the fields of Flanders,
Or the sun squanders
His radiance
And the midges dance
Their day-long life away
Over the green and the grey
Of the fields of France. . . .
And maybe we shall never again
Plod thro' our mire and the rain
Of the winter gloaming,
And maybe we shall never again
See the long, white, foaming
Breakers pour up our strand. . . .
But we have been borne across this land,

And we have felt this spell. . . .
And, for the rest.

L'*Envoi*

What is love of one's land?
                    Ah, we know very well
It is something that sleeps for a year, for a day,
For a month, something that keeps
Very hidden and quiet and still,
And then takes
The quiet heart like a wave,
The quiet brain like a spell,
The quiet will
Like a tornado, and that shakes
The whole being and soul . . .
Aye, the whole of the soul.

[24/12/17 – 1/1/18]

TRISTIA IV. 'THAT EXPLOIT OF YOURS . . .'
[THAT EXPLOIT OF YOURS]

I meet two soldiers sometimes here in hell.
The one, with a tear in the seat of his red pantaloons
Was stuck by a pitchfork,
Climbing a wall to steal apples.

The second has a seeming-silver helmet,
Having died from the fall of his horse on some tramlines
In Dortmund.

These two,
Meeting in the vaulted and vaporous caverns of hell,
Exclaim always in identical tones:
'I at least have done my duty to Society and the Fatherland!' . . .
It is strange how the cliché prevails.
For I will bet my hat that you who sent me here to hell
Are saying the selfsame words at this very moment
Concerning that exploit of yours.

ON HEAVEN
To V.H.; who asked for a working Heaven

That day the sunlight lay on the farms,
On the morrow the bitter frost that there was!
That night my young love lay in my arms,
The morrow how bitter it was!

And because she is very tall and quaint
And golden, like a *quattrocento* saint,
I desire to write about Heaven;
To tell you the shape and the ways of it,
And the joys and the toil in the maze of it,
For these there must be in Heaven,
Even in Heaven!
For God is a good man, God is a kind man,
And God's a good brother, and God is no blind man,
And God is our father.

I will tell you how this thing began:
How I waited in a little town near Lyons many years,
And yet knew nothing of passing time, or of her tears,
But, for nine slow years, lounged away at my table
    in the shadowy sunlit square
Where the small cafés are.

The Place is small and shaded by great planes,
Over a rather human monument
Set up to *Louis Dixhuit* in the year
Eighteen fourteen; a funny thing with dolphins
About a pyramid of green-dripped, sordid stone.
But the enormous, monumental planes
Shade it all in, and in the flecks of sun
Sit market women. There's a paper shop
Painted all blue, a shipping agency,
Three or four cafés; dank, dark colonnades
Of an eighteen-forty *Mairie*. I'd no wish
To wait for her where it was picturesque,
Or ancient or historic, or to love
Over well any place in the land before she came
And loved it too. I didn't even go
To Lyons for the opera; Arles for the bulls,

Or Avignon for glimpses of the Rhone.
Not even to Beaucaire! I sat about
And played long games of dominoes with the *maire*,
Or passing *commis-voyageurs*. And so
I sat and watched the trams come in, and read
The *Libre Parole* and sipped the thin, fresh wine
They call Piquette, and got to know the people,
The kindly, southern people. . . .

Until, when the years were over, she came in her swift red car,
Shooting out past a tram; and she slowed and stopped
    and lighted absently down,
A little dazed, in the heart of the town;
And nodded imperceptibly.
With a sideways look at me.

So our days here began.

And the wrinkled old woman who keeps the café,
And the man
Who sells the *Libre Parole*,
And the sleepy gendarme,
And the fat *facteur* who delivers letters only in the shady,
Pleasanter kinds of streets;
And the boy I often gave a penny,
And the *maire* himself, and the little girl who loves toffee
And me because I have given her many sweets;
And the one-eyed, droll
Bookseller of the *rue Grande de Provence*, –
Chancing to be going home to bed,
Smiled with their kindly, fresh benevolence,
Because they knew I had waited for a lady
Who should come in a swift, red, English car,
To the square where the little cafés are.
And the old, old woman touched me on the wrist
With a wrinkled finger,
And said: 'Why do you linger? –
Too many kisses can never be kissed!
And comfort her – nobody here will think harm –
Take her instantly to your arm!
It is a little strange, you know, to your dear,
To be dead!'

But one is English,
Though one be never so much of a ghost;
And if most of your life have been spent in the craze to relinquish
What you want most,
You will go on relinquishing,
You will go on vanquishing
Human longings, even
In Heaven.

God! You will have forgotten what the rest of the world is on fire for –
The madness of desire for the long and quiet embrace,
The coming nearer of a tear-wet face;
Forgotten the desire to slake
The thirst, and the long, slow ache,
And to interlace
Lash with lash, lip with lip, limb with limb, and the fingers of the hand with
    the hand
And . . .

You will have forgotten . . . .
                    But they will lie awake;
Aye, all of them shall awaken
In this dear place.
And all that then we took
Of all that we might have taken,
Was that one embracing look,
Coursing over features, over limbs, between eyes, a making
    sure, and a long sigh,
Having the tranquillity
Of trees unshaken,
And the softness of sweet tears,
And the clearness of a clear brook
To wash away past years.
(For that too is the quality of Heaven,
That you are conscious always of great pain
Only when it is over
And shall not come again.
Thank God, thank God, it shall not come again,
Though your eyes be never so wet with the tears
Of many years!)

II
And so she stood a moment by the door
Of the long, red car. Royally she stepped down,
Settling on one long foot and leaning back
Amongst her russet furs. And she looked round . . .
Of course it must be strange to come from England
Straight into Heaven. You must take it in,
Slowly, for a long instant, with some fear . . .
Now that *affiche*, in orange, on the kiosque:
'*Seven Spanish bulls will fight on Sunday next*
At Arles, in the arena' . . . Well, it's strange
Till you get used to our ways. And, on the *Mairie*,
The untidy poster telling of the *concours*
De vers de soie, of silkworms. The cocoons
Pile, yellow, all across the little Places
Of ninety townships in the environs
Of Lyons, the city famous for her silks.
What if she's pale? It must be more than strange,
After these years, to come out here from England
To a strange place, to the stretched-out arms of me,
A man never fully known, only divined,
Loved, guessed at, pledged to, in your Sussex mud,
Amongst the frost-bound farms by the yeasty sea.
Oh, the long look; the long, long searching look!
And how my heart beat!
                              Well, you see, in England
She had a husband. And four families –
His, hers, mine, and another woman's too –
Would have gone crazy. And, with all the rest,
Eight parents, and the children, seven aunts
And sixteen uncles and a grandmother.
There were, besides, our names, a few real friends,
And the decencies of life. A monstrous heap!
They made a monstrous heap. I've lain awake
Whole aching nights to tot the figures up!
Heap after heaps, of complications, griefs,
Worries, tongue-clackings, nonsenses and shame
For not making good. You see the coil there was!
And the poor strained fibres of our tortured brains,
And the voice that called from depth in her to depth
In me . . . my God, in the dreadful nights,
Through the roar of the great black winds, through the sound of the sea!

Oh agony! Agony! From out my breast
It called whilst the dark house slept, and stair-heads creaked;
From within my breast it screamed and made no sound;
And wailed. . . . And made no sound.
And howled like the damned. . . . No sound! No sound!
Only the roar of the wind, the sound of the sea,
The tick of the clock. . .
And our two voices, noiseless through the dark.
O God! O God!

(That night my young love lay in my arms. . . .

There was a bitter frost lay on the farms
In England, by the shiver
And the crawling of the tide;
By the broken silver of the English Channel,
Beneath the aged moon that watched alone –
Poor, dreary, lonely old moon to have to watch alone,
Over the dreary beaches mantled with ancient foam
Like shrunken flannel;
The moon, an intent, pale face, looking down
Over the English Channel.
But soft and warm She lay in the crook of my arm,
And came to no harm since we had come quietly home
Even to Heaven;
Which is situate in a little old town
Not very far from the side of the Rhone,
That mighty river
That is, just there by the Crau, in the lower reaches,
Far wider than the Channel.)

But, in the market place of the other little town,
Where the Rhone is a narrower, greener affair,
When she had looked at me, she beckoned with her long white hand,
A little languidly, since it is a strain, if a blessed strain, to have just died.
And, going back again,
Into the long, red, English racing car,
Made room for me amongst the furs at her side.
And we moved away from the kind looks of the kindly people
Into the wine of the hurrying air.
And very soon even the tall grey steeple
Of Lyons cathedral behind us grew little and far

And then was no more there. . . .
And, thank God, we had nothing any more to think of,
And thank God, we had nothing any more to talk of;
Unless, as it chanced, the flashing silver stalk of the pampas
Growing down to the brink of the Rhone,
On the lawn of a little chateau. giving onto the river.
And we were alone, alone, alone. . . .
At last alone. . . .

The poplars on the hill-crests go marching rank on rank,
And far away to the left, like a pyramid, marches the ghost of Mont Blanc.
There are vines and vines and vines, all down to the river bank.
There will be a castle here,
And an abbey there;
And huge quarries and a long white farm,
With long thatched barns and a long wine shed,
As we ran alone, all down the Rhone.

And that day there was no puncturing of the tyres to fear;
And no trouble at all with the engine and gear;
Smoothly and softly we ran between the great poplar alley
All down the valley of the Rhone.
For the dear, good God knew how we needed rest and to be alone.
But, on other days, just as you must have perfect shadows
        to make perfect Rembrandts,
He shall afflict us with little lets and hindrances of His own
Devising – just to let us be glad that we are dead. . .
Just for remembrance.

III

Hard by the castle of God in the Alpilles,
In the eternal stone of the Alpilles,
There's this little old town, walled round by the old, grey gardens. . . .
There were never such olives as grow in the gardens of God,
The green-grey trees, the wardens of agony
And failure of gods.
Of hatred and faith, of truth, of treachery
They whisper; they whisper that none of the living prevail;
They whirl in the great mistral over the white, dry sods,
Like hair blown back from white foreheads in the enormous gale
Up to the castle walls of God. . . .

But, in the town that's our home,
Once you are past the wall,
Amongst the trunks of the planes,
Though they roar never so mightily overhead in the day,
All this tumult is quieted down, and all
The windows stand open because of the heat of the night
That shall come.
And, from each little window, shines in the twilight a light,
And, beneath the eternal planes
With the huge, gnarled trunks that were aged and grey
At the creation of Time,
The Chinese lanthorns, hung out at the doors of hotels,
Shimmering in the dusk, here on an orange tree, there
    on a sweet-scented lime,
There on a golden incription: 'Hotel of the Three Holy Bells,'
Or 'Hotel Sublime,' or 'Inn of the Real Good Will.'
And, yes, it is very warm and still,
And all the world is afoot after the heat of the day,
In the cool of the even in Heaven. . . .
And it is here that I have brought my dear to pay her all that I owed her,
Amidst this crowd, with the soft voices, the soft footfalls,
    the rejoicing laughter.
And after the twilight there falls such a warm, soft darkness,
And there will come stealing under the planes a drowsy odor,
Compounded all of cyclamen, of oranges, of rosemary and bay,
To take the remembrance of the toil of the day away.

So we sat at a little table, under an immense plane,
And we remembered again
The blisters and foments
And terrible harassments of the tired brain,
The cold and the frost and the pain,
As if we were looking at a picture and saying: 'This is true!
Why this is a truly painted
Rendering of that street where – you remember? – I fainted.'
And we remembered again
Tranquilly, our poor few tranquil moments,
The falling of the sunlight through the panes,
The flutter forever in the chimney of the quiet flame,
The mutter of our two poor tortured voices, always a-whisper
And the endless nights when I would cry out, running through
    all the gamut of misery, even to a lisp, her name;

And we remembered our kisses, nine, maybe, or eleven –
If you count two that I gave and she did not give again.

And always the crowd drifted by in the cool of the even,
And we saw the faces of friends,
And the faces of those to whom one day we must make amends,
Smiling in welcome.
And I said: 'On another day –
And such a day may well come soon –
We will play dominoes with Dick and Evelyn and Frances
For a whole afternoon.
And, in the time to come, Genée
Shall dance for us, fluttering over the ground as the sunlight dances.'
And *Arlésiennes* with the beautiful faces went by us,
And gypsies and Spanish shepherds, noiseless in sandals of straw,
      sauntered nigh us,
Wearing slouch hats and old sheep-skins, and casting admiring glances
From dark, foreign eyes at my dear. . . .
(And ah, it is Heaven alone, to have her alone and so near!)
So all this world rejoices
In the cool of the even
In Heaven. . . .

And, when the cool of the even was fully there,
Came a great ha-ha of voices.
Many children run together, and all laugh and rejoice and call,
Hurrying with little arms flying, and little feet flying, and little
      hurrying haunches,
From the door of a stable,
Where, in an *olla podrida*, they had been playing at the *corrida*
With the black Spanish bull, whose nature
Is patience with children. And so, through the gaps in the branches
Of jasmine on our screen beneath the planes,
We saw, coming down from the road that leads to the olives and Alpilles,
A man of great stature,
In a great cloak,
With a great stride,
And a little joke
For all and sundry, coming down with a hound at his side.
And he stood at the cross-roads, passing the time of day
In a great, kind voice, the voice of a man-and-a-half! –
With a great laugh, and a great clap on the back,

For a fellow in black – a priest I should say,
Or may be a lover,
Wearing black for his mistress's mood.
'A little toothache,' we could hear him say; 'but that's so good
When it gives over.' So he passed from sight
In the soft twilight, into the soft night,
In the soft riot and tumult of the crowd.

And a magpie flew down, laughing, holding up his beak to us.
And I said: 'That was God! Presently, when he has walked through the town
And the night has settled down,
So that you need not be afraid,
In the darkness, he will come to our table and speak to us.'
And past us many saints went walking in a company –
The kindly, thoughtful saints, devising and laughing and talking,
And smiling at us with their pleasant solicitude.
And because the thick of the crowd followed to the one side God,
Or to the other the saints, we sat in solitude.
And quietly, quietly walking, there came before us a woman –
That woman that no man on earth or in Heaven
May not divinely love and prize above
All other women; even above love.
That woman, even she, came walking quietly,
And quietly stood by the table before us,
So near that we could almost hear her breathing.
In the distance the saints went singing all in chorus,
And our Lord went by on the other side of the street,
Holding a little boy,
Taking him to pick the musk-roses that open at dusk,
For wreathing the statue of Jove,
Left on the Alpilles above
By the Romans; since Jove,
Even Jove,
Must not want for his quota of honour and love;
But round about him there must be,
With all its tender jollity,
The laughter of children in Heaven,
Making merry with roses in Heaven.

Yet never he looked at us, knowing that that would be such joy
As must be over-great for hearts that needed quiet;
Such a riot and tumult of joy as quiet hearts are not able

To taste to the full. And then that woman, standing by our table,
So near that we could mark her quiet breathing
And the tranquil rise and fall of her breast beneath the woollen cloak,
And the tender, lovely and mild, dear eyes that looked at my dear –
That woman spoke, in her soft, clear, certain tone:
'It is so very good to have borne a son;
It is sad that you have no child!'

There went by an old man carrying many carven gourds,
And, as if it gave her the thought of a pilgrimage,
'To Lourdes,'
She said, 'is not so very far; go there tomorrow,
And there shall come much joy and little sorrow
With the coming of a son very slender and straight and upright,
With a clear glance, and fair cheeks red and white
With our suns of France,
And a sweet voice, very courteous and truthful;
Surely, you shall rejoice!'
And, as she went, looking back over her shoulder, with eyes
        so sweet, so clear and so ruthful,
'Go there,' she said, 'when you have quietly slept,
And kneel you down upon the green grass sod,
And ask then for your child; my word shall be kept.
For these are the dear, pretty angels of God,
And of them there cannot be too many.'

And so I said to my dear one: 'That is our Lady!'
And my dear one sat in the shadows; very softly she wept: –
Such joy is in Heaven,
In the cool of the even,
After the burden and toil of the days,
After the heat and haze
In the vine-hills; or in the shady
Whispering groves in high passes up in the Alpilles,
Guarding the castle of God.

And I went on talking toward her unseen face:
(Ah God, the peace, to know that she was there!)
'So it is, so it goes, in this beloved place,
There shall be never a grief but passes; no, not any;
There shall be such bright light and no blindness;
There shall be so little awe and so much loving-kindness;
There shall be a little longing and enough care,

There shall be a little labour and enough of toil
To bring back the lost flavour of our human coil;
Not enough to taint it;
And all that we desire shall prove as fair as we can paint it.'
For, though that may be the very hardest trick of all
God set himself, who fashioned this goodly hall,
Thus he has made Heaven;
Even Heaven.

For God is a very clever mechanician;
And if he made this proud and goodly ship of the world,
From the maintop to the hull,
Do you think he could not finish it to the full,
With a flag and all,
And make it sail, tall and brave,
On the waters, beyond the grave?
It should cost but very little rhetoric
To explain for you that last, fine, conjuring trick;
Nor does God need to be a very great magician
To give to each man after his heart,
Who knows very well what each man has in his heart:
To let you pass your life in a night-club where they dance,
If that is your idea of heaven; if you will, in the South of France;
If you will, on the turbulent sea; if you will, in the peace of the night;
Where you will; how you will;
Or in the long death of a kiss, that may never pall:
He would be a very little God if he could not do all this,
And He is still
The great God of all.

For God is a good man; God is a kind man;
In the darkness he came walking to our table beneath the planes,
And spoke
So kindly to my dear,
With a little joke,
Giving himself some pains
To take away her fear
Of his stature,
So as not to abash her,
In no way at all to dash her new pleasure beneath the planes,
In the cool of the even
In heaven.

That, that is God's nature.
For God's a good brother, and God is no blind man,
And God's a good mother and loves sons who're rovers,
And God is our father and loves all good lovers.
He has a kindly smile for many a poor sinner;
He takes note to make it up to poor wayfarers on sodden roads;
Such as bear heavy loads
He takes note of, and of all that toil on bitter seas and frosty lands,
He takes care that they shall have good at his hands;
Well he takes note of a poor old cook,
Cooking your dinner;
And much he loves sweet joys in such as ever took
Sweet joy on earth. He has a kindly smile for a kiss
Given in a shady nook.
And in the golden book
Where the accounts of his estate are kept,
All the round, golden sovereigns of bliss,
Known by poor lovers, married or never yet married,
Whilst the green world waked, or the black world quietly slept;
All joy, all sweetness, each sweet sigh that's sighed –
Their accounts are kept,
And carried
By the love of God to his own credit's side.
So that is why he came to our table to welcome my dear, dear bride,
In the cool of the even
In front of a café in Heaven.

PEACE†

The black and nearly noiseless, moving, sea,
The immobile black houses, all one wall
Pressing us out towards the noiseless sea;
No sounds . . .
And – Thou of the Stars! – beneath the blue-white stars
Small yellow lights upon the moving sea . . .
Moving. . .

IMMORTALITY[†]

AN ELEGY ON A GREAT POET DYING ABROAD

I

We read: You have died at a distance,
And that's all: that is all. But it's queer
That that should be all! You dying so lonely,
The news not striking any ear
With any insistence. . . . It isn't one of those blows
That falls on and mutes
For an instant the hearts, brains or ears
Of any mortal that one knows.
It comes, rather, like a murmur of waves
From a sea
One hears very far in the distance,
Fretting insistently against cliffs, into caves,
A reminder
Of our mortality.

II

Heaven knows, you may well prove immortal
So consummate, consummately handled your prose is,
And your poems the summit of Poetry. Only,
Your death might so well, had you chosen,
Have silenced some brutes
Who deem that the odour and soul of the rose is
Matter to cozen
And barter about. As it is, they shall gloat
And ape and contort all the exquisite words that you wrote
Into gawds one might lay at the feet or the portal
Of their opulent bawds. So your flawless, cold words
Shall hinder
Our poor mortality.

III

Why *couldn't* you have left your pulse unheld
Once: for a moment? Say, as the jaws of the grave
Opened to receive you?
Why wouldn't you
Just for a breath forget to hold

Watchful, advisèd; for ever pausing to frame
The sentence that froze
And shrivelled a thought that was carelessly brave –
The phrases you never could mould enough
Or render cold enough? . . .
Your pulse shall go slow enough and you lie low enough
For ever, to-night when they leave you,
Rigid and cautious and grave,
Underneath mould enough,
In a silent chamber
But never more frigid or cold or containedly grave
Than of old you were, contriving your mayflies in amber. . . .

IV

Ah, why *couldn't* you?
What a scroll, then, we might have upheld
At once! To-day! On the first swift rumour of your death;
Before ever the foreign clay of your grave
Was thrown up to receive you!
A scroll
Brave with the braveness of your fame,
Warm with the warmth of your name!
And, into the cold, shining webs you alone had the knowledge to weave –
You,
Yourself, with a failing, last generous breath
Would have breathed such dyes and such tinctures of gold
That, incarnadined,
Not the most disintegrating autumn wind,
No moth gnawing, nor no eatings up of rust
Should have rendered them tenuous or, like your name
Already filmed with thin dust.

V

                    For that's how it is
Already. You, not yet beneath the earth,
Yet here, at home, you could not find one hearth
To crave your shadow falling from the ingle
Towards the curtains. This is your own land
And your face forgotten! Did you have a face,
Eyes, heart to beat and circulate warm blood

Through chilly limbs? Or, did you have a voice
To make one hearer thrill with joy; a palate
For meats or the juice of the grape? Could you rejoice
Over a little money; did you ever know
The ups and downs of fortune quicken your pulse,
Engage in a wager; yearn for pleasant sin
Live lecherously or contrive delights
From human passions? Were you crossed in love
For a faithless harlot or the faithful wife
Of another's bed? Oh, block of flawless jade,
Had you even a dog to wag its tail for you?
We do not know. . . . I know you aimed at Fame
Consummately. Once I lived with you
Five years, day in day out; and one could gather
So much from your unrevealing eyes and lips.
And whilst you sucked the last few pence from our purses
We know you made towards Immortality
Consummately, by means of unstirred prose
And stirless verses. . . . You may get it yet!
Only!
Will there be a face to look up from your page
Kindly and smiling into young men's eyes?
Or a form that any woman would recognise
And deem it like her lover's. . . . As for us,
We crave to be remembered, warm, in the flesh;
If only as those who beat their wives and soaked
Night-long in taverns; whom the crowing cocks
Heard staggering homewards; bulbous, veined-nosed,
Cut-pursey Falstaffs. . . . I had rather that
Than immortality of your frozen kind!
Yes, even that. . . . The grave is whist and lonely;
One shivers at the image of dry decay
In the roots of the grass. . . . And I have sometimes thought
That if we, being years-long buried, caused to arise
In living minds, shapes of our shoulders, say,
Since once we had great rolling shoulder-blades
And found some Boswell; or if our kindly hands
Seemed to give crusts to beggars, stroke old dogs,
Or carry sonnets to enraptured maids,
So that our vanished faces in our books
Were such as woman thought she recognised,
Deeming them like her lovers', known or imagined. . . .

Then, in our shoulders, drying in the earth,
Our desiccated fingers, fleshless features
A moment's tide of life might run again
And be warm and tickling. . . . Do you take me, you?
Or is the thought too sordid?
                              Only. . . . Only,
Your death that made us think upon our ends
– As, for sure it should do – makes us stretch our hands
Towards that lure of Immortality.
You wrote all your life for Immortality
Of a Parnassian, most impersonal shape.
But we, being bone and sinew, crave a kind,
A human, less erasing sort of grave;
A death less passionless, a shade less blind
Than the great steam-roller you confronted; you
Being no doubt more brave!
              *   *   *
We read: You have died at a distance,
And that's all. That is all. It seemed queer
At first when we learned
That that must be all. You, dying so lonely
Where that foreign river flows
To its foreign sea,
And we, finding the news not strike on the ear
With any insistence;
No mourning hatchment hanging on the portal
Of any mortal that one knows!
Think only,
Heaven knows, you may well prove immortal
Having consummately earned
Your Immortality!

From MISTER BOSPHORUS AND THE MUSES*

[NOTE BY THE AUTHOR: – *The Editor asks for an explanation of this work. Surely he underestimates the intelligence of his readers: for what could be plainer? An English poet here looks at the world. Any English POET!*

Argument and the Editor apart, it may be suggested to the Indulgent Reader that He will get more from a poem if He takes, without seeking explanations, what He gets, revelling merely in dissolving views. Your poet is an inconsequential creature. Reviewing his Time he lacks the capacity for such clear, sustained and trenchant thought as distinguishes those, let us say, who review for The Times. *Yet you may have pleasures from him if you let him, now and again diffuse, and then again shrewd, just burble on. . . .*]

From *Act Two:*
(pp.56-66)

> (*1st Semi-chorus, Female*)
> We offerings bring!
> (*2nd Semi-chorus, Female*)
>   Aye: smoke doomed sacrifice!

BOSPHORUS: What once-loved form is this?
ATHIS: I Athis am,
> Glaucis I am, and little Clio's dam;
> Campaspe I and Cytherea too,
> I, Clytemnestra, once beloved by you!
> And Helen, I whom once you hymned so well,
> Eurydice for whom you went to hell
> I am. In me you see as well
> The dove-eyed Hesper whom you used to tell
> Of far, foam-fretted islands.

BOSPHORUS: I did love
> Thee, Athis, once, long since in ages past!

ATHIS: I whom you set above
> All other women find thee here at last!

BOSPHORUS: But say! Why seek ye this secluded spot!
> In the market-place we sought but found thee not!
> What gifts now bring ye in your outstretched hands?

ATHIS: Sweet soothing herbs gathered in Indian lands!
BOSPHORUS: I do not take your gifts. Here! Worm-crowd, here!
> Take ye these cylinders and make your cheer!
> And as to them ye set the Promethean fire,
> Fill your starved lungs, your fervent thanks suspire!
> (*Chorus of Males*)
> The Gods to each ascribe their various fates:
> Some entering in; some baffled at the gates!

(1st Semi-chorus of Males)
But much bethankëd bard, disclose! Explain!
Why meets this weeping damsel such disdain?
(2nd Semi-chorus of Males)
Her deep-born sighs, her heaving breasts, disclose
Tempestuous grief, intolerable woes!
(Chorus of Females)
Our heaving bosoms and our deep-born sighs
Betray the woe we feel. How stream our eyes!
(1st Semi-chorus of Females)
Our faltering accents, outstretched palms betray.
(2nd Semi-chorus of Females)
More than a modest virgin's wont to say!
(Chorus, Male)
Oh, still their weeping! To their woes give end!
Apollo smiles on the poetic friend!
(1st Semi-chorus, Male)
The Gods to each ascribe a differing lot!
(2nd Semi-chorus, Male)
Some rest on snowy bosoms! Some do not!

BOSPHORUS: At Athis' eyes my flame I first confessed;
Her gold-heeled sandals, her Tyrrhenian vest,
Her marble bosom and her milk-white arms
Conveyed to me a thousand tender charms;
To Athis was my virgin Muse addrest!

ATHIS: Upon the sea-cliff where the cedars grow
He lay, and on my bosom's virgin snow
His locks reclined. He struck the sounding lyre
Till all the rocks re-echoed with his fire
And Sea-nymphs envied and the moon burned low.
(1st Semi-chorus, Male)
In vain for love like that the gods t' importune!
(2nd Semi-chorus, Male)
I never, never had that kind of courting!
(Chorus, Male)
The Gods to each ascribe a various fortune.

BOSPHORUS: From Athis' lips my vagrant Muse disporting
Led me to Glaucis. Then from Glaucis' lips
I sipped the nectar; marvelled at her hips;
Her wheat-hued hair; her chiton's snowy hues;
And Glaucis had the tribute of my Muse!

GLAUCIS:	To my soft side tempestuous came he courting;
	Called me his bride; cast down the milk-white fleece
	In the myrtle-shade; his wooings would not cease
	To the cyther tone till he had loosed my girdle!
	Ah me! Thrice-happy maid! Thrice-blessed myrtle.

(1st Semi-chorus, Male)
Torture us not, mad thoughts of amorous strife!
(2nd Semi-chorus, Male)
Do you suppose she really *is* his wife?
(Chorus)
The Gods to each ascribe a differing life!

BOSPHORUS: Tired of the rustic games of nymph and clown,
The Muse conveyed me to the busy town;
That Cupid mark'd! Sharper than tooth of asp, he
Aimed his keen dart. I burned! I burned! Campaspe
Swayed then my Muse betwixt her smile and frown!

CAMPASPE: He sang: I had the stature of the Queen
Of Pluto's realms; shine of the moon and sheen
Of Juno's diadem; wooed to the flute;
Lascivious wood-notes used and dissolute,
Till with his song he bent me to his purpose!
(1st Semi-chorus, Male)
A city madam! Modesty is *her* pose!
(2nd Semi-chorus, Male)
On some the Gods sweet oils, on some the spur, pose!
(Chorus)
The Gods to each assign a differing purpose!
Have mercy, Bosphorus. Be merciful!
No man can rest and hear your loves to the full!
(1st Semi-Chorus, Male)
Their rounded limbs and thy resounding lyre –
Gods, make us chaste! – have set us all on fire!
(2nd Semi-Chorus, Male)
Inflammatory tones! Alluring bosom!
Friends, hold me back! My morals! I shall lose 'em!

BOSPHORUS: Worm! Beast! Toad! Tortoise! Loathly slug! Fat midge!
(1st Semi-chorus, Female)
You cannot love us all! Dear Bard! Abridge!

BOSPHORUS: Not love you all. You mean to say I age!
(2nd Semi-chorus, Female)
I told you so! You've put him in a rage!

BOSPHORUS: I cannot love you all! Jove make me mild!

Not love! I swear I'll get each one with child
'Twixt now and midnight!
                    (1st Semi-chorus, Female)
                              There you are! He'll do it!
                    (Chorus)
Why did you bring us here? We said we'd rue it!

BOSPHORUS: Not love! The Heavens shall blush at my embraces!
                    (1st Semi-chorus, Female)
My new white peplum!
                    (2nd Semi-chorus, Female)
                              My best Tyrian laces!
                    (Chorus, Female)
He ruins them. . . . Those men have hid their faces!
Poor wretched worms! Have we such meagre arms?
What is the matter with our various charms?
                    (Chorus, Male)
My dear companions! Veil each shuddering head!
                    (1st Semi-chorus, Male)
This is the Minotaur! Alive! Not Dead!
                    (2nd Semi-chorus, Male)
To some the stones; to some the yielding bed
The Gods ascribe!
                    (Chorus, Male)
                              Whose is the heavy tread
That hastening shakes the earth? 'Tis Hercules!
He comes! The lion's mane doth brush his knees!
The vine-leaves in his locks from Omphale's
Intoxicating vineyards by the main!
Tyrrhenian!

HERCULES: Ha! Have I them again!
Girls, where's your shame? Poet, where is your awe?
I charge ye! Move from hence! Respect the law!

BOSPHORUS: Master of Labours! Here's no purpose evil . . .

ATHIS: Great Labour Master! He's the very devil!
                    (1st Semi-chorus, Male)
See their tossed locks! Torn garlands! And their clothes!
                    (2nd Semi-chorus, Male)
And then his language! He has sworn such oaths!
                    (Chorus, Male)
The Gods to each . . .
                    (Chorus, Female)
                              Be silent, Paralytics!

(Chorus, Male)
Injurious Females! We are well-known Critics!
(Chorus, Female)
You by your wails have brought this Godhead here
To interrupt our amours with our dear,
Our Fav'rite Poet!
(Chorus, Male)
       Oh! inconstant ones,
The Gods ascribe to . . .

HERCULES: That, my decent sons,
Methinks I've heard before. Euripides,
I think it is . . .
(Chorus, Female)
      Master of Labours.

HERCULES: Cease!
Three at a time besiege my patient ear!
No more than three at once! Tell me why you're here!
(Tri-chorus: Athis, Glaucis, and Campaspe)
Master of Labours! The great poet here
Did by our eyes and our white bosoms swear
Eternal truth to us!
(2nd Tri-chorus)
      To us!!
(3rd Tri-chorus)
       To us!!

HERCULES: A connoisseur is the great Bosphorus!
(2nd Tri-chorus: Cytherea, Clytemnestra, Helen)
Thanks, Master. We next hearkened to his flame,
Till all too soon the Other Woman came!
Unhappy we!
(1st Tri-chorus)
     And we!
(3rd Tri-chorus)
      Unhappy we!

HERCULES: Wherefore unhappy? Three *most* poets use!
Great poets three times three to inflame their Muse:
(3rd Tri-chorus: Helen, Eurydice and little Clio's dam)
That well we know. But, most unhappy we!
We coming last shared but his poverty!
Not wine but mead, libation to our flames!
No fine-horsed chariots to th' Olympic games!

(1st Semi-chorus, Male)
You hear their words! Libations! Women! Song!
(2nd Semi-chorus, Male)
No poet's purse would run to that for long!
(Chorus)
The Gods to each assign a different moral!

HERCULES: If you continue whispering we shall quarrel!
(1st Semi-chorus)
Hush! He will head us in a nail-pierced barrel!
(2nd Semi-chorus)
And yet! This poet's life was most immoral!
(1st and 2nd Tri-chorus, Female)
The plainings of those three are truly comical!
When he wooed us he was most economical!
A couch of fleece; a belt of straw; some flowers!
Refined! But inexpensive!

HERCULES: Heavenly Powers!
What would these women? Poets can in truth
Give you not gold, but sempiternal Youth!
Why after decades do your locks still grow
Golden like wheat-sheaves and your breasts like snow?
Why shall the charms of Glaucis, Athis, Clio,
Be famed from modern Athens to Ohio
In twice three thousand years?
(Chorus, Female)
                        We know it well
Great seed of Phoebus! Future times shall tell,
Shall picture us. The Topic Films of Pathé's
Shall figure Clytemnestra, Hesper, Athis,
Long since in ages past!

HERCULES: Then why complain!
And wherefore have ye sought this sacred place
Forbid to women and their idle train?
(Chorus, Female)
Godhead! No frown upon a woman's face;
No plaint on ruby lip doth leave a trace!

HERCULES: Then what's your errand? Hastily relate
In words succinct!

BOSPHORUS: This grows monotonous!

(Chorus, Female)
In words succincter we will now rehearse!
BOSPHORUS: I really cannot stand this rhyming verse
Five minutes longer!

(Chorus, Female)
                   Poor, great Bosphorus
Fallen on evil days did leave these climes. . .
BOSPHORUS: No! no! I will not go on finding rhymes!

(Chorus, Female)
Three minutes longer! We will be quite terse!

(Chorus, Male)
We much prefer his rhymes to his blank verse.

(Chorus, Female)
His plays lay unproduced on any stage,
His lyrics, once the wonder of the age,
Unquoted and his epics all unsung,
His name no longer upon every tongue,
His lyre no more the glory of our Times
He emigrated into other climes;
Passed from our arms and from our ken went forth:
We *heard* he'd sought the frozen barbarous North.
BOSPHORUS: That's put the lid on! Rhyming no more venture-ye!
I am dead sick of all this eighteenth-century
Insipid metre!

(Chorus, Female)
Bosphorus, our beautiful,
No more in the market-place we found thee!
Erased thy name from the tablets;
Beside wine-purple seas, forgotten;
The fleece unpressed;
Cyclamens
Faded in the autumn all unplucked by thee
Lustre on lustre;
Our locks ungarlanded by thee;
Forlorn, lack-lustre!
Forgotten the beautiful
Singer!

In the market-place sought we the Tyrrhenian laces,
No more thy twined words;
The clepsyhydra measured out the hours

To the drip of its waters, never to the plucking
Of the ivory lyre!
Forgotten the beautiful
Lyric!

On the Acropolis
Sang other poets. . .

HERCULES: I am of course acquainted
With the historic outlines
Of Athenian poetry.
   (1st Semi-chorus, Men)
To us most painful
This short-breathed division:
   (2nd Semi-chorus, Men)
How get
Into short syllables:
   (Chorus, Male)
Divinities of Argos
Devising to each,
Unnumbered destinies?

HERCULES: The slow years passing,
Lustre melting to lustre,
Take we for granted!
Ray cast now on your reasons
For seeking this sacred
Womanless Wan-waste;
Lawless, licentious,
Gold-seeking, gold-haired,
Willow-waist wantons!

ATHIS: Sudden from sea-ways
Sail swart seafarers
Merchanting manuscripts
Stripe-aye, and star-dight
Mounting the market,
Bellowing: *'Bosphorus!*
Bring Bad Mad Bosphorus'
Million-worth Manuscripts!'

HERCULES: Wherefore this wan-ness?
Manuscripts many
Doubtless in days dead
Poet did pen ye!
So from seafarers

Gold have ye gotten
Gold in galoreness!
(1st Male Semi-chorus)
Awful! His autograph
Vaulting in value!
(2nd Male Semi-chorus)
Dreadful! Disgusting
Degeneration!
(Chorus)
Awfully awkward this
Alliteration.

BOSPHORUS: Right to the dawëning now hastneth ye!
Th' Aprillé' soote of our young Poesie!

ATHIS: Of Athis of Athéns blakkë dolóur
There may none eynë dry be for pittý!
Allas! No writings haddë sche in power!
Corn-huëd lokkës must y-curlëd be;
And butter craveth pergament like snoe,
Small fischës fried y-drying of ther fat:
And broidered sleevës that they lie not flat.
So walken we the meadës like a flower!
(1st Semi-chorus, Men)
This newë vers will slé me utterlie.
(2nd Semi-chorus)
We may the fashion of it not sostenë.
(Chorus)
So biteth it upon the tongë kenë.
By Hevenë Queen! Vers was a fairere maid
With apt alliteration's artful aid!

BOSPHORUS: If you can stand this pace, Labour Dispenser,
I can't much longer. Make them cut through Spenser!

*   *   *

From *Act the Third:*
(pp.85-87)

DUCHESS: You must remember that she, and she alone, has the power to
make Bosphorus write. She must! She shall! *Then*, if we could have our
revenge!
(Clarissa exhibits symptons of lively interest.)
But we must dissemble.

LABOUR MASTER: We must think of some deep-laid scheme. Subtle, deep, indecipherable. I have it. . . . But excuse me, there seems to be something going wrong with the lecture. . . . Of course that pestilent fellow has talked those paper-lunged Intelligentsia down again. He always does. But this appears to be more serious. Listen!

THE VOICE OF 34241: No, you cannot kill poetry. You gentlemen are mistaken in thinking that the essence of poetry is rhyme, metre, apt expression, image.

ORTHODOX INTELLIGENTSIA: Oh! oh! oh!

LABOUR MASTER: That appears to be madness. Does that not appear to you to be madness, Duchess?

VOICE OF 34241: Poetry is immortal because it is the endless chain of the linked expressions of the soul of man. This being a prose age, poetry has taken refuge in prose. The poem that we are living to-day, here and now...

INTELLIGENTSIA: Oh! oh! How can poetry be prose? How can we be part of a poem?

LABOUR MASTER: Mad! mad! How mighty a mind is here o'erthrown.

VOICE OF 34241: You, of course, are ugly, sordid, little, arriviste! But not more ugly, sordid, little, and arriviste than the men who listened to Euripides!

INTELLIGENTSIA: Athens! Running down Athens now! Blasphemy! The Eljin marbles! The Medishi Venus! The enclitic de! Ha! ha! ha! ha!!

VOICE OF 34241: Ugly, sordid, little, of imbecile and discreditable ambitions and aims! Who amongst you has a thought he would not blush to own! But yet, humanity! And the distillation of you – as the distillation from a mash of crushed grapes is wine – the distillation of you is poetry.

INTELLIGENTSIA: U . . . u . . . uuuu! He's going to give us free verse! Free verse! Free love! . . . Free beer! Blasphemy! Death!

VOICE OF BOSPHORUS: The punishment of all poets is death! So I will continue. When I have finished, brothers, you may put me to death. But I shall have finished – do not be alarmed! – long before dawn!

LABOUR MASTER: That man is plainly mad! His words are without sense or sequence. Seize him! Gently! gently! Don't damage his hands! To the arbour! Take him to the arbour! Don't fall over the dog!

CLARISSA: I should suggest that you remove his boots! The first thing they do to a drunk in the Clink is to remove his boots.

LABOUR MASTER: Certainly, madam! Intelligentsia! remove that man's boots! Perhaps you would try your hand with him, Miss Clarissa. (*To her, whispering*) We rely on you to get the manuscript from him! Gently over the bank, miss. That's right. We trust him to you! . . . Now, Duchess! She's gone. I can reveal my plan. It has been burning my lips! SHE MUST GET THE POEM FROM HIM: THEN WE MUST KILL HIM! WE MUST NOT KILL HIM BEFORE HE HAS WRITTEN THE POEM!!

DUCHESS: God! What a brain you have!

CLARISSA: Let us conduct him very gently to the arbour. Gentlemen, bring scented soap, white towels, pure water warmed. Mr 34241, rest on me.

BOSPHORUS: I am all right!

CLARISSA *(to him, whispering)*: You are supposed to be mad. It will tremendously assist us in our escape if you continue to appear mad.

*   *   *

From *Act the Fourth*
(p.103)

On fore-stage to extreme right an immense Rolls-Royce, all its metal parts shining with an improbable brightness. In car: NORTHERN MUSE as DUCHESS; LABOUR MASTER as CHAUFFEUR, in rear seat PAUPER 64209 as MISTER BULFIN. They shade their eyes as if gazing into great distances from a mountain top; shake their heads to indicate that the object of pursuit is not visible, and otherwise denote dismay and ill-temper.)

VOICE OF BOSPHORUS:

But how is it possible that men hold dear,
In these lugubrious places,
This dreary land; the clod-like inglorious races,
The befogged, gin-sodden faces;
The lewd, grim prudery; for ever protracted chases
After concealëd lechery; hog-like dull embraces
Under a grey-flannel sky; un-aired and damp
Like poems a-stink of the lamp:
And the learned bronchitics that vamp
Hodden-grey thoughts all to stamp
Craving tenpence for fourpence
And more pence and more pence
And grudging us our pence!

How is it possible that men hold dear
Our dreary, dripping valleys,
Monotonous misty alleys
Whence dully, drearily sallies
Song of grey sodden birds?
In the air of frightening keenness,
The mists of might-have-been-ness,
The ceaseless, ceaseless greenness,
The thought as thick as curds!

DEDICATION
TO E.J.

When you've attained to high estate
You'll think maybe small beer of this.
I shall be dwindled, you so great
I'll hardly reach your hand to kiss.
And you'll go proudly on your way
Nor think: 'Ronsard m'a célébré!'

But, dear, once walk my place about
Where I lie very still and whist:
Then you shall take these verses out
And say: 'He was no prosodist;
His rhymes are false, his metres twist
Like sinners crippled by the gout.
But ah, his love for me was great
And these ten fingers he has kissed!'

A HOUSE[1]

The House. I am the House!
    I resemble
    The drawing of a child
    That draws 'just a house.' Two windows and two doors,
    Two chimney pots;
    Only two floors.
    Three windows on the upper one; a fourth
    Looks towards the north.
    I am very simple and mild;
    I am very gentle and sad and old.
    I have stood too long.
The Tree. I am the great Tree over above this House!
    I resemble
    The drawing of a child. Drawing 'just a tree'
    The child draws Me!

---

[1]   Text taken from *Poetry* (Chicago), 17 (March 1921).

Heavy leaves, old branches, old knots:
I am more old than the house is old.
I have known nights so cold
I used to tremble;
For the sap was frozen in my branches,
And the mouse,
That stored her nuts in my knot-holes, died. I am strong
Now . . . Let a storm come wild
Over the Sussex Wold,
I no longer fear it.
I have stood too long!
The Nightingale. I am the Nightingale. The summer through I sit
In the great tree, watching the house, and throw jewels over it!
There is no one watching but I; no other soul to waken
Echoes in this valley night!
The Unborn Son of the House. You are mistaken!
I am the Son of the House! –
That shall have silver limbs, and clean straight haunches,
Lean hips, clean lips and a tongue of gold;
That shall inherit
A golden voice, and waken
A whole world's wonder!
The Nightingale. Young blood! You are right,
So you and I only
Listen and watch and waken
Under
The stars of the night.
The Dog of the House. You are mistaken!
This house stands lonely.
Let but a sound sound in the seven acres that surround
Their sleeping house,
And I, seeming asleep, shall awaken.
Let but a mouse
Creep in the bracken,
I seeming to drowse, I shall hearken.
Let but a shadow darken
Their threshold; let but a finger
Lie long or linger,
Holding their latch:
I am their Dog. And I watch!
I am just Dog. And being His hound
I lie

All night with my head on my paws,
Watchful and whist!
The Nightingale. So you and I and their Son and I
Watch alone, under the stars of the sky.
The Cat of the House. I am the Cat. And you lie!
   I am the Atheist!
   All laws
   I coldly despise.
   I have yellow eyes;
   I am the Cat on the Mat the child draws
   When it first has a pencil to use.
The Milch-goat. I am the Goat. I give milk!
The Cat of the House. I muse
   Over the hearth with my 'minishing eyes
   Until after
   The last coal dies.
   Every tunnel of the mouse,
   Every channel of the cricket,
   I have smelt.
   I have felt
   The secret shifting of the mouldered rafter,
   And heard
   Every bird in the thicket.
   I see
   You,
   Nightingale up in your tree.
The Nightingale. The night takes a turn towards coldness; the stars
   Waver and shake.
   Truly more wake,
   More thoughts are afloat;
   More folk are afoot than I knew!
The Milch-goat. I, even I, am the Goat!
The Cat of the House. Enough of your stuff of dust and of mud!
   I born of a race of strange things,
   Of deserts, great temples, great kings,
   In the hot sands where the nightingale never sings!
   Old he-gods of ingle and hearth,
   Young she-gods of fur and of silk –
   Not the mud of the earth –
   Are the things that I dream of!
The Milch-goat. Tibby-Tab, more than you deem of
   I dream of when chewing the cud

For my milk:
Who was born
Of a Nan with one horn and a liking for gin
In the backyard of an inn.
A child of Original Sin,
With a fleece of spun-silk
And two horns in the bud –
I, made in the image of Pan,
With my corrugate, vicious-cocked horn,
Now make milk for a child yet unborn.
That's a come-down!
And you with your mouse-colored ruff,
Discoursing your stuff-of-a-dream,
Sell your birthright for cream,
And bolt from a cuff or a frown.
That's a come-down!
So let be! That's enough!
The House. The top star of the Plough now mounts
    Up to his highest place.
    The dace
    Hang silent in the pool.
    The night is cool
    Before the dawn. Behind the blind
    Dies down the one thin candle.
    Our harried man,
    My lease-of-a-life-long Master,
    Studies against disaster;
    Gropes for some handle
    Against too heavy Fate; pores over his accounts,
    Studying into the morn
    For the sake of his child unborn.
The Unborn Son of the House. The vibrant notes of the spheres,
    Thin, sifting sounds of the dew,
    I hear. The mist on the meres
    Rising I hear . . . So here's
    To a lad shall be lusty and bold,
    With a voice and a heart ringing true!
    To a house of a livelier hue!
The House. That is true.
    I have stood here too long and grown old.
Himself. What is the matter with the wicks?
    What on earth's the matter with the wax?

The candle wastes in the draught;
The blind's worn thin!
. . . Thirty-four and four, ten . . .
And ten . . . are forty-nine!
And twenty pun twelve and six was all
I made by the clover.
It's a month since I laughed:
I have given up wine.
And then . . .
The Income Tax!
The Dog of the House. The mare's got out of the stable!
The Cat of the House. She's able, over and over,
    To push up the stable latch.
    Over and over again. You would say she's a witch,
    With a spite on our Man!
The Milch-goat. Heu! Did you see how she ran!
    She's after the clover; she's over the ditch,
    Doing more harm than a dozen of goats
    When there's no one to watch.
    Yet she is the sober old mare with her skin full of oats,
    Whereas we get dry bracken and heather;
    Snatching now and then a scrap of old leather,
    Or half an old tin,
    As the price of original sin!
Himself. I shall have to sell
    The clock from the hall;
    I shall have to pawn my old Dad's watch,
    Or fell
    The last old oak; or sell half the stock . . .
    Or all!
    Or the oak chest out of the hall.
    One or the other – or all.
    God, it is hell to be poor
    For ever and ever, keeping the Wolf from the door!
The Cat of the House. Wouldn't you say
    That Something, heavy and furry and grey,
    Was sniffling round the door?
    Wouldn't you say
    Skinny fingers, stretching from the thicket,
    Felt for the latch of the wicket?
Himself. You would almost say
    These blows were repercussions

Of an avenging Fate!
But how have we earned them . . .
The sparks that fell on the cornricks and burned them
Still in the ear;
And all the set-backs of the year –
Frost, drought and demurrage,
The tiles blown half off the roof?
What is it, what is it all for?
Chastisement of pride? I swear we have no pride!
We ride
Behind an old mare with a flea-bitten hide!
Or over-much love for a year-old bride?
But it's your duty to love your bride! . . . But still,
All the sows that died,
And the cows all going off milk;
The cream coming out under proof;
The hens giving over laying;
The bullocks straying,
Getting pounded over the hill!
It used to be something – cold feet going over
The front of a trench after Stand-to at four!
But these other things – God, how they make you blench!
Aye, these are the pip-squeaks that call for
Four-in-the-morning courage . . .
May you never know, my wench,
That's asleep up the stair!
Herself [in her sleep] I'll have a kitchen all white tiles;
And a dairy, all marble the shelves and the floor;
And a larder, cream-white and full of air.
I'll have whitewood kegs for the flour,
And blackwood kegs for the rice and barley,
And silvery jugs for the milk and cream.
O glorious Me!
And hour by hour by hour by hour,
On piles of cushions from hearth to door,
I'll sit sewing my silken seams,
I'll sit dreaming my silver dreams;
With a little, mettlesome, brown-legged Charley,
To leave his ploys and come to my knee,
And question how God can be Three-in-One
And One-in-Three.
And all the day and all the day

Nothing but hoys for my dearest one;
And no care at all but to kiss and twine;
And nought to contrive for but ploys and play
For my son, my son, my son, my son!
Only at nine,
With the dinner finished, the men at their wine;
And the girls in the parlor at forfeits for toffee,
I'll make such after-dinner coffee . . .
But it's all like a dream!

Himself. If Dixon could pay! . . . But he never will.
   He promised to do it yesterday . . . But poor old Dicky's
      been through the mill.
   And it's late – it's too late to sit railing at Fate!
   He'd pay if he could; but he's got *his* fix on.
   Yet . . . If he *could* pay –
   God! – It would carry us over the day
   Of Herself!

The Clock in the Room. I am the Clock on the Shelf!
   Is . . . Was . . . Is . . . Was!
   Too late . . . Because . . . Too late . . . Because.
   One! . . . Two! . . . Three! . . . Four!

Himself. Just over The Day and a week or two more!
   And we'd maybe get through.
   Not with a hell of a lot
   Of margin to spare . . . But just through!

The Clock in the Hall. One! . . . Two! . . . One! . . . Two!
   As . . . your . . . hours . . . pass
   I re . . . cord them
   Though you . . . waste them
   Or have . . . stored them
   ALL . . .
   One!!
   Two!!
   Three!!
   Four!!
   Begun!!
   Half through!!
   Let be!!
   No more at all!!
   I am the Great Clock in the Hall!!

Himself. It is four by the clock:
   The creak of the stair

Might waken Herself;
It would give her a shock
If I went up the stair.
I will doze in the chair.
The House.   Sad! Sad!
Poor lad!
I am getting to talk like the clock!
Year after year! Shock after shock!
Sunlight and starlight; moonlight and shadows!
I've seen him sit on his three-legged stool,
And heard him whimper, going to school.
But he's paid all the debts that a proper lad owes
Stoutly enough . . . You might call me a clock
With a face of old brick-work instead of the brass
Of a dial.
For I mark the generations as they pass:
Generation on generation,
Passing like shadows over the dial
To triumph or trial;
Over the grass, round the paths till they lie all
Silent under the grass.
Himself. And it isn't as if we courted the slap-up people . . .
The House. Now does he remember the night when he came from the station
In Flood-year December?
Himself. Or kicked our slippers over the steeple,
Or leaving the whites ate only the yolk.
We're such simple folk!
With an old house . . . Just any old house.
Only she's clean: you won't find a flea or a louse!
We've a few old cows
Just any old cows! –
No champion short-horns with fabulous yields . . .
Two or three good fields;
And the old mare, going blinder and blinder . . .
And too much Care to ride behind her!
The House. I'd like him to remember . . .
There were floods out far and wide;
And that was my last night of pride,
With all my windows blazing across the tide . . .
I wish he would remember . . .
Himself. Just to get through; keeping a stiff upper lip!
Just . . . through! . . . With my lamb unshorn;

It's not
Such a hell of a lot!
Just till the child is born . . .
You'd think: God, you'd think
They could let us little people . . . creep
Past in the shadows . . .
But the sea's . . . too . . . deep!
Not to sink . . . Not . . . sink!
Just to get through.
Christ, I can't keep . . . It's too . . . deep . . .

The Cat of the House. He has fallen asleep. Up onto his knee!
    I shall sleep in the pink.

The House. You see!
His mind turns to me
As soon as he sleeps. For he called me a ship
On my last day of pride,
And he dreams of me now as a ship
As I looked in the days of my pride.
Then, he was driving his guests from the station,
And the floods were wide
All over the countryside . . .
All my windows lit up and wide,
And blazing like torches down a tide,
Over the waters . . .

The Mare [From the cloverfield]. That wouldn't be me!
When I was young I lived in Dover,
In Kent, by the sea. So he didn't drive me.
When I was young I went much faster
Over the sticks as slick as a hare,
With a gunner officers for a master.
And I took officers out to lunch
With their doxies to Folkestone. It wouldn't be me!

The Milch-goat. Munch; munch . . . Munch; munch!
    In the Master's clover . . . But poor old Me!

The Unborn Son of the House. Malodorous Image-of-Sin-with-a-Beard,
    It is time I was heard.

The House. That Christmas night . . .

Son of the House. It would have to be Christmas
    With floods so they missed Mass . . .

The House. Your Dad's never missed Mass
At Christmas! . . .
So all my windows, blazing with light

Called out Welcome across the night.
And the Master's voice came over to me:
'The poor old shanty looks just like a ship,
Lit up and sailing across the sea!'
That was my lad . . .
And another, just as young and as glad,
As they used to be, all, before the war,
Said: 'And all of her lamps have all their wicks on!'
That would be Dickson . . .

Son of the House. My mother, when her pains have loosed her
    And I grown to man's estate,
    Shall go in gold and filigree;
    And I'll be king and have a king's glory . . .

The Rooster. Kickeriko! Kickerikee!
    I am the Rooster!

Son of the House. The Dad, with no hair on his pate,
    Reading my story . . .

The Rooster. I am the Bird of Dawn, calling the world to arouse.
    I, even I, am the cock of the house!

The Skylark. Time I was up in the sky!
    It is time for the dew to dry.
    I am the Bird of the Dawn!

The Nightingale. Time I was down on my nest.
    The moon has gone down in the west:
    Day-folk, goodbye!

The House-dog. Here's our young maid! What a yawn!

The Milch-goat. The houseboy is crossing the lawn
    Under the fir.
    Will he give me a Swede?
    That's the thing I most need!

The House. What a stir! What a stir!
    Did you ever?
    All of a sudden it's day
    With its tumult and fever!
    I must have nodded away!

The Drake. I am the Drake! I'm the Drake.
    We too have been all night awake;
    But making no fuss, not one of the seven of us.
    For our heads were far under our legs
    Drinking the dregs of the lake.
    Therefore my ladies lay eggs,
    Ducksegg green!

The Maid. Where have you hid
  The copper-lid?
  Where on earth have you been?
  Where on earth is it hidden?
Houseboy. I didn't!
Maid. You did!
Houseboy. I didn't . . . I never . . .
Maid. I see you . . .
Houseboy. You never!
Maid. How on earth can I ever
  Cook the pigs' food if I can't find the lid
  Of the copper?
Houseboy. You whopper! I never
  Touched the lid of your copper!
Maid. The lid's lying out in the midden.
  Himself must have took it!
House Boy. So there then! Give over.
  . . . .
Maid. Did you ever! What next!
  Our Master's asleep in his chair!
  I'll wager you never a leg he's stirred
  Since four of the clock, with the cat on his knee!
Postman. This letter's registered!
Maid [To Himself]. Ned Postman wants a receipt in ink . . .
Himself [Opening letter]. To sink . . . No, not to sink!
Maid. It's a registered letter
  The postman wants a receipt in ink for.
Herself [Calling from upper window]. Charley!
  The mare's in the clover,
  Making for the barley.
  She's knocking down the sticks . . .
Himself. It's over –
  We're over this terrible fix
  For a quarter or so!
Herself. And we were in such a terrible fix! –
  And you never let me know!
Himself. Not quite enough to take to drink for . . .
  [To Houseboy.] Fetch the mare from the barley,
  You'd better . . .
Herself. Oh, Charley!
Himself. I said: Not quite enough to take to drink for!
  It was like being master of a ship,

Watching a grey torpedo slip
Through waves all green.
It would have been . . .
And all one's folk aboard . . .
Herself. Yourself! Yourself! You'll surely now afford
Yourself a new coat . . .
And a proper chain and collar for the goat!
Himself. Good Lord!
Yourself! Yourself! You may go to town
And see a show: there are five or six on,
And you can have the little new gown
You said you'd fix on . . .
Herself. But, O Yourself, we can't afford it!
Himself. You've not had a jaunt since the honeymoon . . .
Thirteen months and a day. And very soon . . .
The Unborn Son of the House. I shall so pr[i]nk it and king it and lord it –
Over the sunshine and under the moon . . .
Himself. If Fate be kind and do not frown,
And do not smite us knee and hip,
This poor old patched-up thing of a ship
May take us yet over fields all green,
And you be a little dimity queen . . .
Son of the House. As the years roll on and the days go by,
I shall grow and grow in majesty . . .
Herself. You always say I've no majesty! –
Not even enough for a cobbler's queen!
The House. By and by
They'll be talking of copper roofs for the stye!
The Pigs. We were wondering when you would come to the Pigs!
Yet they say it's we that pay the rent!
Himself. Great golden ships in ancient rigs
Went sailing under the firmament,
And still sail under the sky and away –
Tall ships and small . . .
And great ships sink and no soul to say.
But, God being good, in the last resort
I will bring our cockle-shell into port
In a land-locked bay,
And no more go sailing at all!
Herself. Kind God! We are safe for a year and a day!
And he is so skilful, my lord and my master,
So skilled to keep us all from disaster;

Such a clever, kindly, Working One!
That I'll yet have my dairy with slabs of marble,
A sweet-briar thicket where sweet birds warble,
And an ordered life in a household whereof he
Most shall praise the nine-o'clock coffee;
And a little, mettlesome, brown-kneed One
To lie on my heart when the long day's done . . .
Rooster. Pullets, go in; run out of the sun!
He's climbing high and the hayseed's dun.
I am the Rooster with marvelous legs!
Pullets, run nestwards and lay your eggs.
Herself. For my son; my son; my son; my son!

EPILOGUE

The House Itself. I am their House! I resemble
The drawing of a child.
Drawing, 'just a house,' a child draws one like me,
With a stye beside it maybe, or a willow-tree,
Or aspens that tremble
That's as may be . . .

But all the other houses of all nations
Grand or simple, in country or town,
All, all the houses standing beneath the sky
Shall have very much the same fate as I!
They shall see the pressing of generations
On the hells of generations;
Shall bear with folly; shall house melancholy;
At seasons dark and holy shall be hung with holly;
On given days they shall have the blinds drawn down,
And so pass into the hands –
Houses and lands into the hands
Of new generations.
These shall remain
For a short space or a long,
Masterful, cautious or strong;
Confident or overbold.
But at last all strong hands falter;
Frosts come; great winds and drought;
The tiles blow loose; the steps wear out;
The rain

Percolates down by the rafter.
Their youths wear out;
Until, maybe, they become very gentle and mild.
For certain they shall become very gentle and old,
Having stood too long.
And so, all over again,
The circle comes round:
Over and over again.
And . . .
If You rise on this earth a thousand years after
I have fallen to the ground,
Your fate shall be the same:
Only the name
Shall alter!

BRANTIGORN[1]

What is this I hear them say?
Brantigorn has passed this way
Nor ever spared the time to see
How the world was using me!

I remember a roadside hedge
Where I'd a jug, a loaf and a wedge
Of raucous soul-sufficing cheese:
Brantigorn begged the rind at my knees
And the crusts and the dregs and found them good!

I remember the edge of a wood
And him with a rope about his hood;
I riding by bade them set him free.
But the rolling world has rolled over me!

---

[1] In *New Poems*, 'Brantigorn' appears as the first of 'Two Poems in an Old Manner'. Ford revised the second, 'Auprès de ma Blonde', and incorporated it into the longer dramatic poem 'L'Interprète – Au Caveau Rouge', printed here on pp.147-50.

I remember Gudruna's chamber
Grown with ivy a child could clamber:
Brantigorn meantime held my horse
Craving to mumble the warm wet corpse
And later expressed his deep remorse
For leaving the corpse its beads of amber!

I've watched for weeks in the frozen sallows,
Been near a throne and nearer the gallows,
Whilst he, a-quake by his scrivener's fire
Never once clutched at his heart's desire
But up he went or down he went
For part of a wench or four per cent!

But this I say, and I say it to you,
My lords of March, of Fife and Buccleuch,
Marquis of Nairn and Norronsay:
Watch ye well; beware the day,
Or Brantigorn shall pass your way
Nor ever spare the time to see
How the world is using *ye!*

'RHYMES FOR A CHILD: SEVEN SHEPHERDS'
[SEVEN SHEPHERDS: FOR E.J.]

Seven shepherds herd their sheep
    Down seven sleepy stubble fields;
Seven angels stand and weep
    And say: 'How small the harvest yields!'

Seven grey-beards prate of tillage
    Round the ingle of the inn;
Seven call this age an ill age,
    Seven wave their mugs and sing.

And all the signboards of our village
    Creak as they swing,
Whilst the seven stars above the village
    Twinkle and spin.

TO PETRONELLA AT SEA

To the remotest verges of the sea,
Unto ends of night following day
There shall no refuge be for you and me
Who haste away.

Beyond the furthest stretches of the foam
Beyond the last horizon of the sky
For you and me: for you and me, no home
Waits, quietly.

But in the deep remoteness of the heart,
In the deep secret chambers of the mind,
Hidden, unchanging, secret, set apart –
Beyond the whitest surges of the foam,
Beyond the limitless verges of the wind,
In the deep, tender, quiet places of the heart:
Lo! you, enshrined.

BUCKSHEE; *Poems for 'Haitchka in France* (1931)*[1]

[Buckshee, derived from the universal Oriental *bakschisch*, has no English equivalent. It is a British Army word and signifies something unexpected, undeserved and gratifying. If the cook at dinner time slips three extra potatoes into your meat-can those are buckshee potatoes; if for some thing you are paid in guineas instead of pounds, the odd shillings are buckshee; if you are a little Arab boy alongside a liner and a passenger throws half a crown instead of a florin into the shark-infested water for you to dive after, the odd sixpence is buckshee backschisch. Or if you have given up the practice of writing verse and suddenly find yourself writing it – those verses will be buckshee.]

I. [BUCKSHEE]

I think God must have been a stupid man
To have sent a spirit, chivalrous and loyal,
Cruel and tender, arrogant and so meek,
Gallant and timorous, halting and as swift
As a hawk descending – to have sent such a spirit,
Certain in all its attributes, into this age
Of our banal world.
     He had infinity
Which must embrace infinities of worlds,
     And had Eternity
And could have chosen any other age.
     He had Omnipotence
And could have framed a fitting world and time.

But, bruised and bruising, wounded, contumacious,
An eagle pinioned, an eagle on the wing;
A leopard maimed, a leopard in its spring,
A swallow caged, a swallow in the spacious
And amethystine, palpitating blue:

A night-bird of the heath, shut off from the heath,
A deathless being daubed with the mud of death,
A moth all white, draggled with blood and dew,
'Haitchka, the undaunted, loyal spirit of you

---

[1] The entire sequence, with the exception of 'Coda' was first published in *New English Poems*, ed. Lascelles Abercrombie (London, 1931).

Came to our world of cozening and pimping,
Our globe compact of virtues all half virtue
Of vices scarce half-vices; made of truth
Blurred in the edges and of lies so limping
They will not stir the pulse in the utterance. . . .
From a New World that's new and knows not youth
Unto our France that's France but knows not France,
Where charity and every virtue hurt you,
Oh coin of gold dropped into leaden palms,
Manna and frankincense and myrrh and balms
And bitter herbs and spices of the South. . . .

Because God was a stupid man and threw
Into our outstretched palms, 'Haitchka, you.

II. COMPAGNIE TRANSATLANTIQUE

What a dead year! The sea
Swings, a dull amethyst;
And the doves and sparrows droop
Grey and the gulls in the mist
On the dull wet rim of the sea.

Slowly, slowly, heavily, heavily; dully, so dully, the heavens lower.
Slowly, slowly, heavily, dully, the sands of the hourglass descend.
I have neither foe nor friend;
I am neither erect nor stoop;
I am neither enslaved nor wield power.
Will this endless day never end,
Or this month or this year?
Slow, heavy, dull, drear,
Why should they end? . . .

The mists are riven;
The sea swings free.
There's blue in the heaven
And horns on the sea.

Iô! Iô! the conches blow.

The sparrows and doves
All follow their loves.
The white gulls troop
In a lane on the sea.
There's a horn on the hill!
A furrow is driven
(Though you are invisible still.)
Straight from the sky-line to me.

And
Iô! Iô! the conches blow.
Iô! Iô! 'Ha-*itchka!*

III. FLEUVE PROFOND
   (Nuitée a l'américaine)

   Your brilliant friend
Brilliantly lectures me on the feminine characters
Of my female characters.

   Our striking host,
Having strikingly struck his striking head
Against the bottom panel of his bedroom door,
Has been conveyed to bed
By several combined but unconcerted efforts.

   Hear how he sings . . . .

   The other guests
Dispersed among the apartments of the appartement,
Dazedly hearing the appraisements of Elaine
Concerning half forgotten feminines, I sit
Beside her brilliance on the divan-edge,
My knees drawn up to my chin in the dim light.
We seem to be alone.

   She tosses back
Her brilliant mane and white uplifted chin.
Long throat! Makes incantation with her spidery, white,
Butterfly-moving fingers. I JUST LOATHE
MISS WANNOP

There
Drift sounds of harpsichords,
Of saxophones and ukeleles, drums,
Mandolines, mandragoras, slapped faces, spirituals,
Lacing the Paris night.

That's four o'clock
The Luxemburg clock drones out.

But . . . hear them SING.

Beside her I
Sit like a drummer, peddling rubber pants
And comforters in the Atlas mountain valleys
Beside their largest lion. Knees drawn up
Almost to the chin; peeping, a-shiver, sideways,
At a lip-licking monster. I am all unused
To talk about my books. IF I COULD GET
MY FINGERS ON YOUR ROTTEN CULLY'S THROAT.
She can't mean me. By rights I am the lion!
I'M ALL FOR SYLVIA. Then it's Tietjens' throat
In jeopardy.

But hear them rolling along.

It aint sayin nothin. . . . A black light's shining
It aint doin nothin. . . . Across the shadows
It keeps on rollin. . . . A ray of granite
I LOATHE YOUR TIETJENS. . . . A cone of granite
What's that dark shining? BUT THAT'S 'HAITCHKA
I LOATHE THAT WOMAN. . . . NO, NOT 'HAITCHKA
HOW STUPID OF YOU. . . . THE WANNOP TROLLOP
     MY BEST MOST INTIMATE FRIEND

You too had drawn
Your knees up to your chin. And, motionless,
In an unwinking scrutiny you sat,
A cone of granite, a granite falcon,
A granite guardian of granite Pharaohs.

The leather chair
You'd chosen for your vigils made with you

A cone. Egyptian, chiselled, oriental,
Hard. Without motion. Polished, shining granite.
Did you watch to save your dearest friend from me
Or me from your dearest friend?
                              I wish they'd sing
Another rhythm. You gaze before you.

It must be seven. Are you all going?
Yes, Ezra's going. Not one more hot dog!
The Halles for breakfast.

                    I LOVE YOUR SYLVIA
SHE KEPT HIM JUMPING SHE LOATHED HIS VITALS
SHE GAVE HIM THUMBSCREWS THE CALLOUS MEALSACK
Yes, Marjie's going. Bill ARE you coming?

        I know why *she's* your dearest friend.

Elaine aw COME on . . . 'Haitchka, bring her.
Why, where's 'Haitchka? . . . She's with that writer.
Oh, with that WRITER. Aw, with THAT writer
        She'll keep HIM rolling along.

Schenehaia means 'Pretty creature.'
Schenehaia! For short "Haitchka.'
        She'll keep him rolling along!

IV. CHEZ NOS AMIS

Silent in the background she
Glowers now and then at me
With a smouldering tigress' eye
That does dream of cruelty.

Leopard, ounce or ocelot
She by turns is cold or hot;
She is sinuous and black
Long of limb and lithe of back.

The deep places of the mind
She can probe and thus can find
Every weakness, every blot,
Every weary, aching spot.

She will scrutinise her prey
Turn disdainfully away,
Sinuous and dark and cold.
Then she'll spring and then she'll hold.

Then with what a dreadful heat
She will mangle breasts and feet
And hands and lacerate a heart.
. . . And then listlessly depart.

V. L'INTERPRÈTE – AU CAVEAU ROUGE

They sing too fast for you? I will interpret.
That aged, faded, leonine-faced carle
In dim old tights and frayed, striped gaberdine
Now quavers the famous sonnet. This is it

SONNET DE RONSARD

> *When you are old and dim the candles burn,*
> *Seated beside your fire, with distaffs, gossiping,*
> *And reading out this verse say 'Here's a thing!*
> *Ronsard m'a célébrée du temps que j'étais jeune.'*
> *There shall be no old spinster shall not turn,*
> *Though half asleep above the brands that sing*
> *And, hearing of my name, cry 'Here's a thing!*
> *Ronsard extols our dame from out his urn.'*
>
> *My soul shall wander through the myrtle dust*
> *Of fields Elysian, thou as thou must*
> *Shalt bend, all bent, above the dying brands.*
>
> *Ah, lady, seize the hour the minute flies,*
> *Restort thee thither where thy true love lies*
> *Nor wait till hail torture thy tender hands.*

You did not know I was a poet? Few
Possess that knowledge. I've the trick at times
Give me the subject. I will find you rhymes.
This Provençale, bright-cheeked, high stomachered,
With coal black eyes shall sing a thing. The tune
Might make you cry if you had any heart.

PLAISIR D'AMOUR

> Love's sweets are sweet for such a little day,
> Her bitterness shall last your whole long life.
>
> The world forsook, I followed Sylvia.
> Me now she leaves to be another's wife.
>
> 'Whilst still the waters of this stream shall glide
> Between its banks of meadow-sweet and bracken
> 'Tis thee I'll love.' Thus, thus, once Sylvia cried.
> The waters flow: their verge she has forsaken.
>
> Love's truths are sweet for such a little day!
> Her bitter falsehoods last a whole long life.

Now here's your favourite she's going to sing.
Knowing, it's said, what gentlemen prefer
She's flaxen locked, but once was *brune piquante*
And Prix du Conservatoire. Poor thing, she'll write
Her autograph on your programme if you smile at her.
But she's a lovely voice.

AUPRES DE MA BLONDE

SHE: *Down in my father's garden sweet blooms the lilac tree,*
      Down in my father's garden sweet blooms the lilac tree
      And all the birds of Heaven there nest in company.
HE: Where lieth my leman, blonde and warm and blonde is she
      Where lieth my leman fine it is to be!

SHE: *Down in my father's garden sweet blooms the lilac tree*
      And all the birds of Heaven there nest in company,
      The quail, the speckled partridge, the turtle fair to see.

HE: Where lieth my leman, blonde and warm and blonde is she!
Where lieth my leman fine it is to be!

SHE: *And all the birds of Heaven there nest in company,*
The quail, the speckled partridge, the turtle fair to see;
And eke my pretty stockdove sings night and day for me.
HE: Where lieth my leman, blonde and warm and blonde is she
Where lieth my leman fine it is to be

SHE: *The quail, the speckled partridge, the turtle fair to see,*
And eke my pretty stockdove sings night and day for me.
She mourneth for such fair ones as not yet wedded be.
HE: Where lieth my leman, &c., &c.

SHE: *And eke my pretty stockdove sings night and day for me,*
She mourneth for such fair ones as not yet wedded be,
But I have my fair husband, so mourns she not for me.
HE: Where lieth my leman, &c., &c.

SHE: *She mourneth for such fair ones as not yet wedded be*
But I have my fair husband, so mourns she not for me.
HE: Now tell me this, ah fair one, where may thy true love be?
Where lieth my leman, &c., &c.

SHE: *But I have my fair husband, so mourns she not for me.*
HE: Now tell me this, ah fair one, where may thy true love be?
SHE: *The fause Dutch have him taken, he lies in Batavie.*
HE: Where lieth my leman, &c., &c.

Now tell me this, ah fair one, where may thy true love be?
SHE: *The fause Dutch have him taken, he lies in Batavie.*
HE: What would'ee give my fair one thine own true love to see?
Where lieth my leman, &c., &c.

SHE: *The fause Dutch have him taken, he lies in Batavie.*
HE: What would'ee give my fair one thine own true love to see?
SHE: *Oh I would give Versailles and Paris, that great citié!*
HE: Where lieth my leman, &c., &c.

What would'ee give my fair one thine own true love to see?
SHE: *Oh I would give Versailles and París, that great citie,*
St. Dennis, Notre Dame and the spires of my countrie,
HE: Where lieth my leman, &c., &c.

SHE: *Oh I would give Versailles and París, that great citie,*
     St. Dennis, Notre Dame, all the spires of my countrie,
     And eke my pretty stockdove that sings alway for me!
HE: Where lieth my leman, &c., &c.

VI. CHAMPÊTRE

Yesterday I found a bee-orchid.
But when I gave it you you never raised your eyebrows.
'That a bee-orchid? It's like neither bee nor orchid.'
Was all you said. And dropped it amongst the tea-table debris,
And went on gazing out over the lake,
As once you dropped my letters into a Sixth Avenue garbage can
And went on gazing up West Ninth Street
Towards Wanamaker's.

                  Years ago
We boys went spread out over Caesar's Camp
With the Channel at our backs. In the sun shone,
Across the strip of blue, the pink-blue cliffs of France.
And the wind whispered in the couch-grass
And in the heat of the sun the small herbs' scents were pungent
And sweet and stirring.
And one of us would find a bee-orchid.
From fold to fold of the Downs the cry would go;
'A bee-orchid!' 'Ho! A bee-orchid!' 'Hullo! A bee . . . *orchid!*'
And God promised us the kingdoms of the Earth, and a corner in France
And the heart of an Oriental woman.

Well, here is the corner of France.
The kingdoms of the Earth are rather at a discount,
We should not know what to do with them if we had them.
And you, you have no heart.

VII. RIPOSTES

What did you do in Sodom Town?
How did you sin in Paris?
    I heard the small talk rise and die down
    And thought: 'Her hands are tiny and brown.
    Curse on the time that tarries!'

What did you do twixt then and now,
Since it is past eleven?
    I heard the talk run anyhow
    And thought: 'How brown and broad her brow,
    And her white teeth how even!'

What will you do twixt now and when
You hide 'neath carven marble?
    I do not know; but I know', then
    I'll hear you laugh with gentlemen
    With your laugh like the blackbird's warble.

VIII. VERS L'OUBLI [L'OUBLI – TEMPS DE SÉCHERESSE]

We shall have to give up watering the land
Almost altogether.
The maize must go.
But the chilis and tomatoes may still have
A little water. The gourds must go.
We must begin to give a little to the mandarines
And the lemon trees. Yes, and the string beans.
We will do our best to save
The chrysanthemums
Because you like them. Then, if only another big storm comes
Like the one of Saturday fortnight's
We might just barely do it . . . So
We may get through to the autumn.
At any rate we are through with the season of short nights
And water given at dusk will remain in the earth until
The torrid sun and the immense north wind
They call the mistral once again burn up the face of our hill.

You will find
There will be no change in the weather now until
October. August nearly over, the season of storms is done
Altogether. There will be nothing but this hot sun
And no rain at all
Till well into the Fall.

Till then we must trust to the fruits
Though their trees are dried down to the ends of their roots.
The muscats are done.
The bunch that hangs by the kitchen door is the last but one.
But the wine-grapes and figs and quinces and gages will go on
Nearly till September.
(If you lay down some of the muscat wine-grapes
        on paper on the garret floor
They will shrink and grow sweeter till honey is acid beside them.)

How singular and vocal and sweet those birds' voices are.
For them we may thank the drouth.
Without it they say they never care
To come to us from their woods of the infinitely distant South.

I wish we could have saved more of the plants but
        the weather has tried them
Beyond their endurance. And there is no goodness in our land
On this side of the hill.
Even the wood has hardly enough heart to make fuel
Though with vine-prunings in the winter days –
When the sea below us is like ruffled satin
And the sky an infinite number of subtle greys
And the mistral sings an infinite number of lays in Latin –
And you crouch beside the hearth we shall manage to make up a blaze
To get up and go to bed by. . . . But I like the baked, severe, cruel
Hill with sea below and the great storms sooner or later. And for me
There is no satisfaction anywhere greater
Than is given by that house-side, silver grey
And very high above the sea.
With the single black cypress against the sky
Over the hill
And the palm-heads waving away at the mistral's will.

Well then:
We have outlived a winter season and a season of spring

And more than one season of harvesting
In this land
Where the harvests come by twos and threes
One on the other's heels.
Do you remember what grew where the egg-plants and chilis now stand?
Or the opium poppies with heads like feathery wheels?
Do you remember when the lemons were little and the oranges
    smaller than peas?
We have outlived sweet corn and haricots,
The short season of plentiful water and the rose
That covered the cistern in the time of showers
And do you remember the thin bamboo canes?
We have outlived innumerable growths of flowers,
The two great hurricanes
And the innumerable battlings back and forth
Of the mistral from the Alps in the north
And of siroccos filled with the hot breath
– 'Sirocco that man unto short madness hurrieth!' –
From the sands of Africa infinite miles to the South.

And having so, ephemeral, outlived the herbs of the hill
We may maybe come through the drouth
To the winter's mouth
And the season of green things
And flowering cisterns and springs.

Hark at the voices of those birds in the great catalpa's shade
Hard by the hole where the swifts once made
Their nest on the rafter, thrilling all through the night.
Singular birds with their portentous, singular flight
And human voices. They came all the way
Over the sea to the bay
From Africa.
It is only our drouth that could have lured them away
So far from the South. It was perhaps they
Ulysses took for the syrens calling: 'Away!'
When he took shelter here from the thunderous main.
And perhaps we may never again
Hear their incomparable, full resonance
Compact of wailing and indifferent mirth
And undecipherable, honeyed laughter
Or not on this earth under this torrid sun.

For they say
It is only once in a century they come this way
In time of drouth from their eyries far to the South
In Africa.

Or perhaps we shall hear them only after,
All harvest gathered in and the time of all fruits being done,
We – oh but not too severed in time nor walking apart –
Shall pluck and cry the one to the other along the folds of Cap Brun
'The Herb Oblivion!'

For this is a corner of France,
And this the kingdoms of the earth beneath the sun,
And this the garden sealed and set apart
And that the fountain of Jouvence. . . .
And, yes, you have a heart.

LATIN QUARTER [CODA][1]

1
Two harsh, suspended, iron tocsin notes
Reverberate panic from that clock of Richelieu.
They throw athwart the unconcerned night,
Over the warren that's our black purlieu
Their unavailing tones of harsh, unheeded fright;
They pour through the pellitory of the wall that grows
Over the mouldering stones
Their droning overtones. . . .

Prolongedly shuddering these say:
    'Be alarmed! Your hours are wasting away.
    Your life approaches its last day.
    Rise! Take arms against Chronos that will not stay.
    And, armed, await the day!'

---

[1] [Ford added the following note when he collected this poem:
*Written in the rue de Seine for an anniversary between the feasts of SS.
James & Paul (Otherwise May Day) & That of Saint Joan of Arc.*
                                        MCMXXXVI]

But the velvety, black
Night with her myriad fingers floats back.
She stifles the notes in the bells' throats;
Her velvet silences obliterate
The scars from her velvet pall.

2
Through it all you sleep and the fingers of the darkness
Feel ceaselessly my brows,
Your cheeks, my shoulders uncovered,
Your uncovered hands, my throat. . . .
The velvety fingers of the deep night.

As far as one knows
It is almost only here that the night shows this solicitous note
Of quietly, blindly, feeling the uncovered skin. . . .
As if to make sure that the tenants have all come in,
Not loitering in black streets to sin,
Nor too liquored up to find their locks,
Nor too disturbed by the hourly repeated shock
Of reverberated panic from Richelieu's old clock
And all the other wheezing, churring, murmuring old clocks
Of our learned Quarter that drowses beside Seine water.

3
I suppose
This is our final stamping ground. We may never leave again
This mouldering triangle that mounts gradually from the Seine
Up to the mouldering Luxemburg on its mound . . .
Our last abiding place and territory
For it is not only that here you find pellitory of the wall
Pushing its dowdy flowerets through the patina
That falls in a thin dusty film and covers
All Richelieu's *Quarta Latina*
And its unvarying *status quo ante*. . . .

It is obvious that we must have patina and dust.
We are the sort that must, since our brain
Will not work in the atmosphere of the perfect Drain
And Cellophane. And we must
Live in irregular perspectives drawn in crumbling stone
Running upwards into times long gone

And yet so passionately here. . . . We must
Hear Names and Affairs and old passions by which to adjust
The mind and get into perspective
Our era of plumbing and planes,
Of the maniacal passion of invective,
Of execration between nation and nation
In a gigantic monotone.

4
Yet it is not merely that Dante
With his as yet unmerited aura,
Pondered in these streets or that Héloïse
Here confronted the summer breeze.

There have been hecatombs of other lovers
Who lie now, silent in forgotten tombs. . . .
Petrarch and his Laura
In the Vaucluse; and Tristan and his Isolde
In old Almaigne; and Copperfield and his Dora
In middle-old, middle-class Cokaigne;
And Vogelweid and Fru Holde
And the innumerable troubadours with their
        unnumbered and immortal loves,
Voicing the Muse
Of the great plain of the Bouche
Du Rhone with its olive groves.

    (Yet, don't forget, here dwelt Heine with his Mouche
    Shaking all Almaigne
    With the scorn born here in his brain
    On midnight mattresses of unending pain.)

5
And elsewhere, as here,
Have been droves of other illustrious
Poring other lore by their midnight stoves,
Pondering in philosophers' groves
To the cooing of Athene's doves.

(And above all, of your courtesy, do not forget those
        bespectacled industrious
    Inventing on co-operative sixes and sevens

To the croaking of Thor's raven,
Iron and mephitic cataclysms
To send through the pitchy abysms
Of the tocsin-riven heavens,
For the eradication of this haven from Earth's face.)

6
But we are here because this place is a haven.
We have found a haven in this place.
Here hath the Lord given the harbourage
Which, when we strode, bemired, over the winter roads
Beneath too heavy loads,
Or rode, dog-tired, the outrageous and malignant seas,
We had desired.

The Earth here turns slow on its axis
And Time, grown tired
Of the review of ages on the heels of ages,
And seasons on seasons
Here leans on his elbow, at ease
Beside our unrestless tide.

The very taxis
Glide
Noiseless and slow
Through the dark streets below,
And your sleep is dreamless and deep
And your pulse is unfevered and slow
Nor do you moan in your sleep
As you did some years ago.

7
To Hell with Richelieu's bell!
It lies in its throat.
Time does not here hasten away,
There is no regular division here
Of night into day
Nor here does our Sphere
Turn on its bored old axis
To the tune of seasons, irrevocable
And told by rote.

8
Listen! The lying clock
Marks three and the drowsing night
Blankets its notes in their flight;
Nevertheless the shuddering overtones exclaim:

  'There shall flame cargoes of fright through the night
  Above this town; the heavens shall be riven;
  Chariots of blazing doom shall be driven
  Across the waste-places of Heaven.
  Your mansions shall crumble down
  And your ashes be entombed in dust that was doomed
  In the first-written sentences of God's
  Because here Knowledge springs from the Earth
  That was accurst before grass grew on sods,
  Knowledge having her head for ever against God's
  Own image's heels.'

9
It sounds well enough, that sort of stuff!
It's a half-truth.
Sure, if there be a spot where frugal thought,
A liking for the arts, knowledge, temperate learning,
Some sort of just appreciation for the worth
Of life, and pity and moderation naturally grow
Like pellitory of the wall on crumbling stones,
Then, sure, be very sure, if its fame spread a little about the earth,
You will find all mankind in hordes without ruth . . .
Bankers and tailors, soldiers, pimps, sailors and tinkers . . .
All mankind with flint-axes and arrows,
Torches, powder, cannon, swords, gas-shells and bombs
Crowding the road in wains, flying together in planes tow'rds that
    detested focus.
All crying together from their planes: *'Bedamn to their hocus-pocus!'*
Razing the buildings, cutting the throats of the thinkers,
Rifling their tombs,
Driving great steam-ploughs to level the ground,
With great harrows harrowing in salt by the ton,
Then wiping their brows and crying: 'That is done.
There shall never again grow the herb called Thought
In this land of oblivion.'

10
But there's more than that in it. . . .
. . . Wait a minute!
Slowly across the blackness of the wall
Glimmer a square and a scroll . . .

That's not poetic imagery; those
Are all my past and all your promises
Illumined by a taxi rolling below.
The one's my roll of proofs like Michelangelo's
Scroll of the Fates on the Cumæan lap.
And the pale square's your *Spring in the Luxemburg*.
Like his table of your Law on Moses' knees.

I know you don't like Michelangelo.
But the Universe is very large with room
Within it for infinities of Gods
Peaceful and co-existent, much as you and I
Here drudge, engrossed, with paper or on canvas,
You in that corner, I in this,
With thoughts going side by side for years,
Fortnights, Millennia, Æons. . . . Thought
Being immensurable and yet commensurate. . . .

11
For you cannot measure time or thought by the time-piece.
It can't be done. You can measure meals or cloth
Or railway-journeys, cornfields or the sea
By dials, and yet not Eternity
That's Time grown incorruptible, nor Thought
That's Life transmuted into rustless gold.

That is not truly hard to understand.
Not really. . . . Imagine honeycomb
Boxed as you see it on your market-stalls. . . .
Some fifty boxes, row on row over row
In a parallelogram. Your eye selects
Box three, row one: then that's alive for you.
                                    But, should your glance
Pass to row four, box nine, box three doesn't die
Though you don't see it. . . . Immortality
Is not more strange than that. Time boxes up

His honey like your apiculturist.
But it most be honey, not *ersatz* bee-bread
That sullen bees chew out on wasted days,
When flowers lack. For Bee-Man Time exacts
A certain flowering, a fertilization,
The stir of life through pollen on the pistils.
I think they're pistils. . . . Then you see Corruption
Don incorruptibility and Time
Put on the Immortal. . . . Surely for every man,
For you, for me, for Heine, for the milk-girl,
Dry, desert tracts must lie athwart the road,
Unmarked, unchronicled, remembered only
As dull malaises lie at the back of the mind.
For Dante's aura was unmerited
Till he met Béatricë . . . so he says
And the tale's writ well enough. . . . So let it pass
For us. We'll leave out the deductions.

To-night the rusty, iron-tonguëd bell
Of Richelieu's clock æons ago strikes one,
An hour past shall strike three; in a century
Shall strike some more or did not strike at all.
But what's the odds? My pompous scroll, your square,
Both faded when the taxi-cab went on
Towards its own eternity. We are
Again suspended in our velvet blackness,
Afloat on questing fingers; we're in a haven
Of fertile hours; we listlessly shall lie
Till doomsday or the end of hostilities,
Whichever prove the longer. . . . Or till you moan:
'Oh, hell, I've got to finish this damn canvas!'
And I clutch groaning the preposterous record
Of my dead, desert footsteps. . . . Silence falls
For a millennium of unheeded clocks,
And you say; 'What's for dinner?' and old Time
Dons incorruptibility and Life's
Immortal. The untimely sun shines in
And you must drop your brush, Praxiteles
Having grown jealous.